WORLD OUT OF WORK

Giles Merritt

COLLINS
St James's Place, London
1982

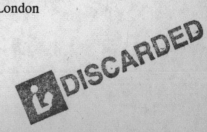

William Collins Sons & Co Ltd
London · Glasgow · Sydney · Auckland
Toronto · Johannesburg

British Library CIP data
Merritt, Giles
  World out of work.
  1. Unemployment – Social aspects
  2. Unemployment – Economic aspects
  I. Title
  331.13'791812   HD5701

First published 1982
© Giles Merritt 1982
ISBN 0 00 216634-8
Photoset in Times
Made and Printed in Great Britain by
William Collins Sons & Co Ltd Glasgow

CONTENTS

ACKNOWLEDGEMENTS

When researching *World Out of Work* I was fortunate to visit Japan, the United States and many European countries, where I was able to interview a broad spectrum of political leaders, top businessmen, trades union chiefs, bankers and academic experts. I shall not attempt to list them all, and some would not wish me to. But I should like to thank the following for their time and advice: Christopher Brooks, Bernard Bruhnes, Ian Byatt, Peter Coldrick, Richard Cooper, Ivor Crewe, John Evans, Lydia Fischer, Eli Ginzberg, Max Kaase, Skip Kasdorf, Magda Lambert, David Lea, Ray Marshall, Dieter Mertens, Franco Modigliani, John Morley, Len Murray, Michael Piore, James Prior, Graham Reid, Martin Rein, Ivor Richard, Jacques Rigaudiat, Günther Schmid, Rob Shepherd, Michael Steed, Gary Stern, Lester Thurow, Eric Varley, Endymion Wilkinson, Robert Worcester.

I owe a special debt to Claudia Downing, without whose efforts my documented research would have been skimpy, and to Juliet Bourgouin. My particular thanks, too, to Malcolm Downing for his scrupulous reading and editing of my draft typescript. The task of indexing the book was greatly lightened by my wife, Pamela, and my sincere thanks too to Patricia Kelly for her help.

This book could not have been written without the support of my newspaper, the *Financial Times*, and its Editor, Geoffrey Owen. Just as crucial has been the forbearance and friendly encouragement of my colleagues in Brussels, John Wyles and Larry Klinger. Were it not, however, for the enthusiasm, stamina and active support and advice of my wife it would never have been started, let alone finished.

1

The Blighted Generation

It is a cruel irony that the tens of millions of young Europeans destined to search fruitlessly for work in the 1980s were born into an age of unparalleled prosperity and optimism. Their birthright was to have been greater economic wealth and sounder social progress than that achieved by their parents. Instead, most stand to inherit uncertainty and distress.

The changes in their fortunes occurred, largely unnoticed, before many of them had even entered their teens. These were structural shifts in the European, and other Western industrialized, economies. More galling, perhaps, to the workless youth of this decade will be the fact that their age and lack of privilege will prevent them taking any great hand in improving matters. They may riot, they will certainly be bitterly resentful, but they are an impotent generation.

For the 'baby boom' children of the 1960s were not only healthier and more numerous than previous generations, they were many of them born with outsized silver spoons in their mouths. As it was the new post-war wealth of Western Europe that had suddenly lifted birthrates, much was lavished on the new generation. Fast rising educational standards were just a part of a general social progress in Europe that set new horizons for the children's expectations.

Those hopes are now being dashed. Over 8 million school-leavers will be seeking employment in the Common Market countries alone during the first half of the 1980s, and their chances are on average much the same as in Britain, where during 1982 only one youthful job hunter in three is likely to succeed.

The sheer size of the sixties 'baby bulge' is an important factor. But it alone is not responsible for the worsening worldwide jobs crisis. Even now, however, all too little is known about the new phenomenon of mass unemployment. Is it a short term, cyclical problem? Or is it, as seems probable, a long term, structural upheaval?

The unanswered questions do not stop there. The international character of the new unemployment phenomenon itself throws up a host of dangerous unknowns.

If a lack of work were just another symptom of the lingering British disease, the remedies would be that much simpler. But all the great industrial nations are being stricken in varying degrees. Some politicians have even drawn comfort from that, though the reality is that international competition for jobs is becoming a serious threat to stability and peace. The world's richest countries may be all in the same boat when it comes to unemployment, but it is unlikely that they will look on it as a grim experience to be shared with stoicism. They are more liable to start by quarrelling over the iron rations and finish by eating one another.

The trigger for turning today's trade tensions into tomorrow's *casus belli* is most probably the level of domestic trouble created for each country by unemployment. If the social and political pressures build up to intolerable levels, then the safety valve of war risks becoming an attractive option for some governments.

The possibility that those pressures could become so great still seems remote. For to most people unemployment looks little different to what it always was: a small minority of the workforce out of their jobs for varying lengths of time, and currently made worse than usual by recession. Largely unobserved, though, or at any rate unrecognized, the nature of unemployment has changed.

Until not so very long ago, few people were out of work for long. And the social security benefits designed to tide them over while in between jobs ensured that there was little genuine hardship. Now, when people go out of work they tend to stay out of work. The jobs crisis is creating a new class of underprivileged people, and proving to be a divisive force in countries whose broad twentieth century commitment has been to greater social and economic equality.

Before the new unemployment took hold, joblessness could be used as a classic instrument for tuning economies. It was standard to brake the rate of inflation at the cost of marginally higher unemployment. Now the dole queues are acting as a parachute drogue jerking whole economies to a crawl. The jobs crisis is one that is rapidly getting out of hand, and the dawning suspicion is that there can be no upturn in jobs. Failing industries are collapsing just at the point when young people, the product of the 1960s baby boom across Europe, are seeking work in unprecedented numbers.

Overlaying that unfortunate coincidence is the issue of new technology that is rapidly overturning the traditional structure on which industries have been built – machinery is for the first time becoming a cheaper commodity than manpower. What the effects of that will turn out to be is the subject of heated debate amongst the economists. There is a compelling intellectual argument that the micro-chip's efficiencies will produce cheaper goods, and because those goods will then come within the reach of so many more consumers the whole cycle of production/consumption will eventually pick up speed. The empirical evidence so far supplied by the industrialists, however, is far from encouraging. Millions upon millions of jobs in both manufacturing and office services are already in the process of being suppressed in the industrialized countries by micro-electronic equipment, and some analysts say that is only the shadow of worse to come.

*   *   *

'Has the Prime Minister been told?'

The question came almost as an afterthought as I was getting up to take my leave of a senior man at the Department of Employment.

We had been talking of the worsening jobs crisis and of his belief that the anger of the hardcore unemployed would reach a fever pitch of street violence in the mid-1980s. It was late June, 1981 and the rioting in almost 30 British towns and cities then lay only days ahead. We were unaware of it but that month was the deceptively calm eye of the storm; the flames of Brixton had begun to die down but Toxteth had yet to burn.

'Oh yes', he answered, perhaps a little glumly as he looked out over Tothill Street in Westminster to the empty, scaffolded shell that had until recently housed the Confederation of British Industry, 'she knows all right.'

I loitered to delay leaving. It had been a question more or less at venture, but the reply was intriguing. Until then I had assumed that Mrs Thatcher was unaware of the real dimension of the jobs crunch, had not been fully briefed on the perils that will accompany high and rising unemployment in Britain and around the world. And even if advice had been proffered, I supposed it must have gone unheard. What, I wondered, would a briefing for Mrs Thatcher have consisted of? Did the civil servants risk speculation or did they stick to measurable facts that could be even more misleading still? Were the briefings concerned with crisis measures or did they examine longer term implications?

Perhaps the briefing was a military style 'sitrep'. 'The areas ringed in red, Prime Minister, are socio-economically deprived inner-city districts where our intelligence suggests that youth unrest has reached a point at which attacks on the police can be expected at any moment. Chief Constables concerned have been alerted and have placed their forces on stand-by. At this juncture we would recommend limiting reaction to most of the standard counter-insurgency techniques we employ with success in Ulster – perhaps not rubber bullets but certainly water cannon, and we propose instructing Special Branch to step up its infiltration efforts.'

Or would it have been a more soothing economic analysis? 'The U/V ratios in principal manufacturing centres – I beg your pardon, Prime Minister, that's the number of registered unemployed in relation to the number of notified job vacancies – have yet to return to pre-recession levels. But, if school-leavers are discounted, the local Jobs Centres report a perceptible slow-down in the upward unemployment trend for the summer months.'

Maybe it was a futurologist's report. 'You will appreciate, Prime Minister, that of necessity our conclusions must be regar-ded as tentative. But Scenario I for 1995 gives us a picture of the major cities being pretty well run down by then. Mainly blacks and unemployed, of course. Only a few million people working in the new greenfield manufacturing operations, and the service activities around them have in employment terms been rather drastically pruned by micro-technology. Education looks to be the great divide. You'll see from the full report in front of you how the poverty line rose steadily during the eighties to overtake almost everyone who hadn't at least a full secondary education.

'Scenario II is rather grimmer, I'm afraid, PM. In 1995 the economy is still getting some boost from all the post-war reconstruction work – you'll find the detailed stuff on the protec-tionist trade wars of the eighties, and how they triggered the hostilities, in Annexe "C", Prime Minister – but our poor R & D effort and low investment since the seventies means we are now having to import most of the key equipment we need. We're providing work for other countries and unemployment is on the rise again.'

*   *   *

Some governments in Europe *do* fear that unemployment may one day, as in the 1930s, lead to war. France is now urging a framework of international financial co-operation on a scale not seen since the US Marshall Plan funded the rebuilding of Europe following World War II. But the instinct of most political leaders, including Margaret Thatcher, has been to play down the implications of the jobs crisis even though it is emerging as the dominant theme of the 1980s.

Has there been a form of cover-up? Not in the strict sense of the term, as the multiplying size of the dole queues cannot be hidden. But if the use of political power to divert attention away from the issue and to discourage examination of how serious the unemployment problem is becoming has not been a cover-up it has at least been a smokescreen.

Governments are deeply uncertain, and internally divided, about the implications of the jobs crisis. Their response has been to play it down rather than confront it, so that in France key forecasts were suppressed in 1979. In America today, the Reagan administration's bland confidence that it will get 3 million people back to work by the mid-eighties is confounding the sceptics and forcing some of Wall Street's toughest analysts on to the defensive.

Governments can do much to deny credibility to those whose warnings are unwelcome, and they can also influence independent opinion. Inside international bodies that were set up to identify priorities and help shape policies, notably the world's 24 rich industrial countries' Organisation for Economic Co-operation and Development (OECD), the refusal of some of the most powerful member governments to admit that unemployment has developed into the most pressing economic problem of all has been silencing the alarm bells. The watchdogs are being muzzled by their owners.[1]

Has Mrs Thatcher then been covering up? Not even her sternest critics accuse her of the Nixon touch, just a Nelsonian preference for holding the telescope to the wrong eye. Refusing early in 1981 in the House of Commons to lend any credence to warnings of 3 million unemployed before the year was out, when she had apparently been advised that such a figure was almost inevitable, was perhaps symptomatic of what trades union chiefs like TUC Assistant General Secretary David Lea refer to as 'an element of cover up'. In other words, the government chooses to see the jobs crisis as no more than a short term difficulty. The spotlight is deliberately trained on next quarter's unemployment figures when it is the trend leading to next year's levels and beyond that is the more significant.[2]

Analysis of unemployment is, in any case, far from being a precise science. As unemployment itself is a miasma of different elements, the 'headline' totals of people in the dole queues released monthly by governments and bannered in the newspapers provide no more than a rough and ready guide to what is happening inside the economy. Sometimes the crude figures can be downright misleading, as in the closing months of 1981 when the apparent jobless total in the UK suddenly stalled just short of the 3 million mark. By the beginning of 1982 it became evident that there had been no real slackening in the trendline of the jobs crisis, just a technical, and seasonal, hitch in the registration of newly unemployed.

That the terms unemployment and joblessness are antonyms is probably significant. Except in the acting profession, where 75 per cent of actors can be 'resting', work is the normal state. The absence of work is a much less clearcut concept, and its economic and social characteristics are far from straightforward, which is why there is room for so much contradictory and confusing argument. Beneath the broad mantle of unemployment, people can be out of work for just a short while, or forever; they can choose to be jobless, or be discouraged from jobseeking; they can move in and out of the formal, registered labour market faster than a computer can count; they can earn a living that makes a contribution to the economy, and still be unemployed as far as the taxman is concerned; and they can muscle other people out of the labour market.

Some OECD experts believe that these shades of grey that make analysis so difficult are a major problem. They inhibit diagnosis and so are delaying prescription and cure. They believe that an important advance would be to establish an international convention for grading unemployment, in much the same way that different definitions are now applied in the area of money supply.[3]

Grading unemployment, and making the phenomenon less opaque, looks a good idea. Unemployment One, or U1, could supply the headline figure of registered jobless, while the other gradations would provide an at-a-glance guide to what is taking place beneath the U1 surface. In that way, U2 might be the measurement of long-term unemployed, those without work for more than six months, who are the core of the jobs crisis because they have a 1-in-10 chance of regaining a job. If U3 were youth unemployment, and perhaps U3b were black or immigrant youth unemployment, then the conditions that create social and political unrest might leap into sharper focus. Add U4 as the measure of those people who are estimated to be discouraged, and therefore outside the labour market, and the dimension of the unemployment problem would be more readily apparent.

Unemployment, in all its guises, may well go to around 5 million people in Britain alone by the mid-80s, and if it does the advent of the micro-chip in both offices and factories could make it hard for that unemployment level ever to be much reduced. Work is becoming a precious commodity. In the Common Market there will be at least 12 million officially unemployed by 1985, and more probably 15 million. Taking the OECD industrialized countries as a whole, joblessness is now only two-thirds of its way towards the 35 million people mark that some experts expect by mid-decade.

Those are the comparatively conservative estimates. There are others that are truly frightening; so much so that they tend to be dismissed as scare projections because their implications are almost impossible to absorb. But then scare tactics would no doubt have been attributed to anyone who during the darkest days of the 1974 recession had been bold enough to forecast a doubling of the then OECD unemployment total to 20 million people by the end of the seventies and a figure of 23 million by 1981.

European trade union analysts are now warning that 1985 could see a jobless total in the EEC alone of 18 million, and that takes little account of the high technology revolution.[4] Studies lately conducted into the job depredations that micro-electronics are capable of suggest that between 35 and 70 million people in the Common Market countries will be somehow affected in the next ten years or so. Whether that means they could lose their occupations permanently, or will be pushed out of work temporarily while re-adapting nobody can yet tell. Work is anyway going to become so scarce that by the mid-80s, before the microchip begins to bite really hard, unemployment will have become one of the most widely shared conditions outside the usual human experiences such as birth, hunger, sex, death and so on. A sixth of Europeans will be unemployed, a third will have had recent experience of unemployment and the lives of 80 per cent will have been touched by joblessness among friends or family. For the OECD countries, one projection cited recently in an Economist Intelligence Unit report on the jobs crisis pointed to a staggering 65–70 million people out of work before the mid-1990s. It did not claim that that politically insupportable level would be reached, it merely pointed out that with the accelerating use of new technology if productivity increases a bit faster than output then it well could.[5]

Jobless forecasts for industrial nations pale besides those for the Third World. There are now at a rough guess 300–500 million unemployed in the developing world, and by the turn of the century the demographic figures suggest 900 million or possibly 1 billion people.[6]

What has gone wrong? It still seems only yesterday that full employment was one of the foundation stones of post-war Western society. And even today many people imagine that it will be again once the recession is past.

A short-cut through the reasons for industrial decline now being put forward is the rather fatalistic suggestion that the world is in the unshakeable grip of a 'Kondratieff Cycle'. It is a theory that the rhythm of economic activity moves in stop-go cycles of about a quarter of a century – an upswing of 20–25 years followed by a downswing of much the same length. When the Russian economist of that name first identified these cycles back in the 1920s – before disappearing forever into one of the Gulags during a Stalin purge – he was able to trace a fairly consistent pattern well back into the nineteenth century. Fast growth mar-

red only by shallow recessions from 1851–73, slow growth exacerbated by deep recessions from 1873–94, a return to boom
conditions during what is always said to be the golden twilight
before the Great War and then the slump conditions of the
inter-war years. Posthumously, Kondratieff was also proved
right by the post-war growth years up to 1973. So now his theory,
which had for long received scant attention, is being dusted off
and economic stagnation is said to be the main feature of the
years up to the mid-1990s.[7]

It is an intriguing theory, in its way not unlike the one that
observes that all Presidents of the United States who win office in
rounded years of a score or its multiple – Abraham Lincoln 1860
right through to Jack Kennedy 1960 – die in office. The snag with
Kondratieff is not his impeccable track record but the way in
which wars also punctuate his cycles. Political disorder throughout Europe in 1848, followed soon after in the early 1850s by the
Crimean War in which France and Britain fought Russia. Then
the Franco-Prussian War of 1870, a slew of colonial wars waged
by different European powers in the 1890s and finally two world
wars. More war by the end of the 1980s?

One can play all sorts of games with these patterns, and it is
about as instructive as having Gipsy Rose Lee as a political
advisor. There is not, for instance, anything very useful to be
deduced from the fact that World War I was followed by economic slowdown and that World War II ushered in a period of
sustained economic growth. Yet wars nevertheless do have a
significance. In economic terms the build up to them and their
duration is often just what the doctor ordered. American economists point to the unhappy coincidences of peacetime and jobs
shortages during the past 50 years: a depression from 1929–40
then war and full employment, recession in 1949 then the boost
of three years of Korean War until 1953, more recession in 1954
and in 1957–8 and again in 1960–1 and then the Vietnam War
from 1965–73.[8]

Nuclear weaponry, of course, makes war a highly unattractive
proposition; although one could wish that military reappraisals

of the feasibility of 'tactical nukes' were not coinciding with a decade in which international tensions must inevitably increase. The doctrine of Mutual Assured Destruction, or MAD, looked a more efficient coolant than the 'window theory' that has brought European theatre missiles into vogue.

The mainspring of war is trade: it is nations squabbling over markets for their goods, over sales that make the difference between unemployment that a government can live with and mass unemployment, that threatens political instability. The classic response, when international competition becomes unendurably tough, is protectionism – either in the shape of tariffs and quotas to protect a country's domestic market, or in the form of subsidies that help to give its industries an edge in foreign markets.

Almost all advocates of protectionism advance it as a purely temporary measure, yet it is, by its nature, a habit forming drug that needs to be taken in ever larger doses. If, behind tariff walls, motor cars are being produced at a higher price than outside, their inflated price tag must stimulate inflation. All the goods that go into a car become more expensive, and their suppliers less internationally competitive. As a result, they need more protection than ever.

The unpalatable fact is that, whatever most industrial countries choose to do, they will be losing jobs. Refusal to fall into the trap of protectionism will also see employment levels drop as industries are forced to become more competitive. But opting to be less competitive, which is what protectionism means, entails far greater long term job losses. By the same token, failure to embrace new technology as fast as possible means handing over the sharpest industrial edge yet devised to competitors elsewhere. Yet in developing micro-technology ourselves we are, in traditional employment terms at any rate, voluntarily cutting our own throats. It is fair to say that, over the last 100 years, the electromechanical equipment developed more or less retained a constant handicap in relation to human labour. On average, however sophisticated it became, its cost was up to 100 times greater than manpower. In other words, it had to perform a function that men could not readily do, or that it would cost 101 men to do. That relationship will soon be gone forever.[9]

So far, micro-technology is no more than a mixed blessing. Mainly, it performs old tasks more efficiently, without throwing up many new tasks. In a world where we live by buying and selling things, high technology has so far done little more than make those things less valuable. Really new inventions, as distinct from more efficient techniques for producing old ones or variations of old ones, are few and far between. The nineteenth century saw the birth of the motor car and of aviation and laid the foundations of telecommunications technology. Between them, those industries provided an industrial dynamic for the twentieth century. The micro-chip has yet to do that.

Almost four-fifths of an industrialized country's economy is made up of wages – what people pay one another for processing goods or providing services adds up to a delicately balanced and crucially important economic structure. Understandably, the fear is that until the micro-chip produces a new dynamic, as did railways in the nineteenth century and motor transport in the twentieth, it will merely devalue work.

The new Luddites of the micro-electronics era point to forecasts that up to a third, or even two-thirds, of all factory and office jobs could be suppressed, or at least radically changed, by the new technology within ten years or so. They warn that if those people are not employed in the economy, then they will not be able to buy in it either.

Yet it may be, for all that, that far too much is being made of the negative aspects of the dawning micro-chip revolution. The example of economies like that of Japan, where high productivity has apparently ensured low unemployment, is strengthening the hand of those who argue that the latterday Luddites have fallen headlong into one of the most basic traps of economic theory. It is claimed that they have swallowed, hook, line and sinker, what is known as the 'lump of labour' fallacy.

Broadly, it is that they are making the cardinal mistake of thinking that there is only a limited amount of work to be done, and failing to realize that if goods can be produced much more cheaply then many more people will be able to buy them. In that way, it is said, the micro-chip will eventually speed up the economic merry-go-round.

The debate between these two camps – those who maintain that the new micro-electronic technology is destructive of labour, and those who believe that all improved technology is regenerative – is likely to rage for years. Not least because there are so many important contributory factors to confuse the issue.

There is, for a start, the international question hanging over the development of the micro-chip in industry. It is a form of technology that is not only becoming cheaper at an accelerating rate, so that developing economies can afford to instal it, it is also particularly well suited for use by unskilled labour when directed by highly qualified technicians. It could well be that micro-electronics eventually generate higher levels of production; but will that new work be enough to satisfy the industrial countries' job needs? As users, the developing countries, with their combination of lower wages and fewer trades union restrictions, seem better placed than the industrialized countries that are currently the producers of the technology.

There is also the question of the goods and services that will become available to so many more consumers. What precisely will those products be? An example sometimes used by those who warn against the lump of labour fallacy is that, as the price of a television set falls, more people can afford to buy a video-recorder as well. It is possibly a rather revealing example, for it demonstrates very simply the force of the argument that cheaper goods stimulate demand, but seems to acknowledge the limited range of products at present susceptible to that. It is hard to see the micro-chip rapidly yielding economies on the goods and services that make up a household's principal outgoings – public and private transport, housing and energy, food and drink.

A further point, that is far from resolved, is the degree to which demand for many consumer goods has become saturated in the developed western economies. Motor car manufacturers see running costs resulting from higher oil prices as a factor that is depressing demand, but also point to the fact that their domestic markets are nowadays made up mainly of replacement buyers, and therefore are expanding at a much slower rate than when there were many first-time buyers. Running counter to that, and supporting the view that consumers' appetites are far from blunted, is the evidence of cheaper cars from Japan and Eastern Europe that have created their own demand.

Increased productivity is a double-edged sword. Belgian industry, which exports rather more than half its output, has since 1970 improved its productivity by a Japanese-style 90 per cent-plus. It has maintained its share of vital export markets in Western Germany and Holland, but has also jumped to the top of the EEC's league table for unemployment. Instead of a constant number of workers producing an increased volume of goods, the reverse has happened. It has remained competitive because a decreasing number of workers have been producing a roughly constant volume of goods.

An anecdote that reveals the other side of the productivity coin, and is directly relevant to the micro-electronics issue, is told by Ray Marshall, the former US Secretary of Labor in the Carter administration. 'If the American banks were to provide the same range of customer services as they now do, *without* any of the office technology that since World War II has made those improvements possible, then they would need to employ every single adult woman in the United States.'[10]

The main drawback to the idea of micro-electronically-boosted productivity as a solution to the jobs crisis, however, is speed. The speed of the baby boom generation's disruptive impact on Europe's labour markets, coupled with the fast-accelerating speed of the micro-chip's attack on traditional working practices, makes it unlikely that the European countries can absorb those twin shocks. Speed has already become the hallmark of the jobs crisis, if the rapidity of industrial collapse, the growth of long term and youth unemployment and the overtaking by events of the joblessness forecasts is any guide.

Those Fallible Forecasters

There is a time bomb inside the OECD. Not a crude explosive device to shatter the dignity of that international organisation, although its headquarters in a leafy side street of the smart 16th arrondissement in Paris once witnessed a bloody terrorist siege in the early 1970s, but a scrap of paper bearing the figures 35,000,000.

For officials in the Secretariat of the Organisation for Economic Co-operation and Development, the combined think tank and economic negotiating forum for the Western world's 24 most developed nations, are now pondering a confidential in-house prediction that by 1985 OECD unemployment will have risen uncontrollably to total 35 million people. That means it will be more than twice as high as ten years before and a full third greater than the crisis levels of the early 1980s.

OECD officials are generally a cautious breed. The political constraint of acting sometimes as servants and sometimes almost as masters to member governments in the economic policymaking field makes them so. Trades union representatives linked to OECD in an advisory council called TUAC warned in mid-1981 that joblessness in the 24 countries would total 30 million by 1982, and despite its inner reservations the Secretariat's reaction amounted to a Mandy Rice-Davies retort – 'Well they would say that, wouldn't they?' The OECD's public declarations have so far been limited to a warning that during the middle part of 1982 joblessness in the OECD area will hit 25–26 million people. That alone draws a sharply rising graph that for many governments represents political dynamite; the line lifts gently enough across the squared paper from the 1975 figure of 16·5 million up to 21 million by 1980, then shoots sharply up to 23 million at the end of 1981 and rises almost vertically to 28·5 million-plus in 1982. And that is before it takes off towards a dizzying 35 million only three years on.

There is no conspiracy of silence preventing the release of such estimates, just a palpable awareness inside the OECD that it would be unwise to set in train the machinery that would produce that 35 million figure as an official projection. OECD figures often move markets and discomfit governments, and because of that are sometimes arrived at only after 'consultation' with a member country. Therefore the limitations of a medium term forecast over such a wide area as all OECD unemployment, where the final figure risks being a million or so out either way, are a discouragement. But they would also be a fairly minor obstacle if OECD governments were pressing for such a forecast. Of course they are not, for in almost all those governments the fight against inflation is identified as the prime objective and the publication of OECD figures demonstrating the scale of the jobs crisis, and emphasizing that the worst is still to come, would spell serious political trouble for them.

It is, no doubt, an ostrich-like tactic for many of those governments to adopt. Ignoring an economic upheaval of the dimension of the unemployment problem while in office seems a guaranteed way of being put out of office. Paris has already a cautionary tale to tell of the unwisdom of suppressing joblessness forecasts.

Across the River Seine on the Left Bank, a twenty-minute taxi ride from the OECD headquarters, lies the heartland of French government, the ghetto of ministerial offices contained in discreet town houses lining the rue de Varenne and surrounding the Prime Minister's Hotel Matignon. During 1979 and 1980 a bureaucratic tussle was played out between those offices over worrying unemployment projections for the country, and its outcome had a direct bearing on President Giscard d'Estaing's election defeat in the spring of 1981. French government economists working on the preparation of the country's Eighth Plan, the blueprint for economic management from 1981–5, had warned more than two years before the elections that joblessness was already getting out of hand. Their predictions had been hurriedly buried by Prime Minister Raymond Barre, chiefly because they were irreconcilable with his anti-inflation plan.

It was, by all accounts, a galling experience for the technocrats of the economic planning side who make up the cream of the French administration. For their computer projections, using the INSEE econometric model, showed that the country's employment position was deteriorating at a much faster rate than anyone had imagined. When the print-out was analysed, it indicated that France's registered unemployment would by 1985 have jumped to 2·25 million, over a million people more than in late 1979, and that the country was by then a year to eighteen months further down the slippery slope leading toward mass unemployment than was realized. The 1960s baby boom generation was known to be creating pressure on jobs but it had since become evident that industrial collapse was rapidly making France's jobs gap unbridgeable. The suppressed analysis showed that 330,000 people risked joining the dole queues yearly; 230,000 of them youthful entrants to the labour market and a further 100,000 yielded by the disappearance of jobs. The computer model had been deliberately constructed in such a way that people who had no job but who did not show up on the registered unemployment figures would also be estimated. The answer was that, to the 2·25 million jobless figure, another 'hidden' third should also be added.

The facts are too recent for history to relate whether Valery Giscard d'Estaing and his Elysée Palace officials knew and approved of the burial of what at that time seemed 'scare' forecasting. But by the closing months of 1980 it had already become plain that it was a political error of the first magnitude, and, by early 1981 in the run-up to the election, it was evident that unemployment had become the single greatest threat to

Giscard's re-election chances. He pointed to the fact that there were actually more people in work than when he took office in 1974 – though only marginally, up from 17·25 million to 17·8 million – and by April he had identified joblessness and the 1·6 million people already on the dole as 'France's No. 1 problem'. He promised 1 million new jobs by 1985, but it was too late.

It would also have been too little. In common with almost all unemployment projections so far the scare figures that had earned Raymond Barre's displeasure soon turned out to be short of the mark. France's new government under Francois Mitterand now believes that without its sharp change in policy, in which jobs have top priority, the figure for 1985 would be 2·5–3 million. The extent to which it can make an impression on those figures, its officials concede, still remains to be seen. By the winter of 1981–2, they had topped the 2 million mark.

In those instances where either the date or the jobless total forecast has already been reached, the forecasters' record has been dismal. Even the trades union economists, who were widely suspected of piling on the agony to further their own ends, have been proved ultra-conservative by a jobs crisis that has gathered a momentum of its own. In September 1980 the European Trade Union Institute, the research arm of the trade union movement grouping for Western Europe, warned that by 1985 Western European joblessness would reach 9 million and added the further caution that it could 'tear apart the fabric' of society. Unemployment for those countries sailed past the 9 million point in the early months of the following year. Prognos, the Basle-based consultancy that does a lot of corporate and governmental work in the jobs forecasting field, has been equally overtaken by events. In 1979 it caused something of a stir with a report putting Western European unemployment at around 10 million by 1983, with 8·7 million jobless in the European Community. The Prognos figures were passed well before the end of 1981, so that by early 1982 it was the EEC, rather than all Western Europe, that had a total of over 10 million jobless.

In Britain, the forecasters have fared no better. The National

Institute for Economic and Social Research announced in August 1980 that by the end of 1981 joblessness in the country would have reached 2·19 million. The ink was scarcely dry on the pages of its report before that level was reached at the turn of the year, and the National Institute hurriedly produced an update setting 3 million by the end of 1982 as its revised estimate. That in turn was overtaken a year ahead of schedule, while Warwick University's Manpower Research Group had similarly set 3 million as a peak unemployment figure but chose 1983 and so was two years out.

Econometric models, the carefully selected sequences of assumptions and variables recreating the economic knock-on effects of different policies, have yet to cover themselves with glory in the unemployment forecasting game. One widespread problem seems to be that they are too 'stiff', their structure as a computer programme is too inflexible to cope with vital new factors such as the revolution in micro-electronic technology. Others are said to be 'too Keynesian', and so presumably find it hard to ponder monetarist policies. HM Treasury's econometric model, which is used to analyse the likely effects of a given government policy and is often pointed to as a model-maker's masterpiece, has limitations that are quite revealing. It cannot distinguish between government spending on health and its spending on defence, nor can it distinguish between grants paid to different industries or even separate regions. But perhaps the computerized model's greatest difficulty has been in coping with developments that have come together to produce an almost chemical reaction. Recession and the collapse of manufacturing industry have coincided with the arrival on to the jobs market of the baby boom generation born in the early 1960s. The combination is not only politically and socially explosive but also threats an economic nightmare.

In the EEC alone, the five years up to 1985 will see about 8 million youthful jobseekers arriving on to the labour markets of the member states. Britain in fact gets off fairly lightly, with a working age population (those between 15 and 64 years old) jumping from 35·8 million in 1980 to 37 million in 1985. In West

Germany there is a 2 million increase to 42 million; it is similar for Italy where it goes from 36 million up to 38 million, and for France where it was 34 million and reaches 36 million. In Holland the problem is even more acute, for 9 million in 1980 leaps to 9·6 million by mid-decade and about 10 million by 1990. These working age population figures tend to exaggerate the difficulty, for a working age population is not at all the same thing as the working population or labour market – in the UK the former may be over 36 million now but the latter is less than 26·5 million. They do nevertheless give an idea of the demographic bump that will cause such havoc in Europe throughout the 1980s.[1]

What is surprising is that the demographers in the European countries most affected do not appear to have given very effective warning of this tsunami wave of humanity that was rolling silently toward the jobs market. If they rang alarm bells, they were either too small to be heard or governments refused to listen. Yet during the 1970s the United States had been swamped by an even taller tidal wave, resulting from a sustained baby boom that began immediately after World War II and which, by the time it finished in 1965, had totalled 75 million births. Its peak had been during the spreading prosperity of the 1950s, so that throughout the 1970s North America as a whole (Canada having been similarly blessed) was forced to create around 20 million new jobs of varying durability. The lesson of what a baby boom can do to an economy may not have been well learned by Europeans, but it is one that Americans have now taken very much to heart. Now that the disruption of the first baby boom is almost over – the pig having passed through the python, as the saying goes – US demographers are warning of the 'echo effect' that will produce a second baby boom there around the turn of the century. By 1985 a third of the US population will be made up of that baby boom generation and will produce a second concentration of births. American planners are already stressing that schools, for example, should be temporarily converted to other uses but not closed; a point that should be considered in Europe where by 1990 there will be a quarter fewer school age children than in the late 1970s, but only for a while.

While the US was struggling heroically to create employment for the new jobseekers of the seventies, Europe and Japan were also having to contend with tough new pressures on employment. They used the same broad economic technique as the Americans, and in doing so may well have expended all their ammunition on shooting at the vanguard of unemployment and are now left defenceless before the main army. For the shot that almost all the leading OECD nations fired, in varying amounts, against joblessness in the 1970s was productivity. They traded efficiency for jobs.

From 1973–9 the EEC countries saw with some disquiet that unemployment levels were edging upwards, but they managed to hold the line with total employment remaining roughly constant in spite of their economic vicissitudes. Those jobs in industry that went under were made good by the creation of 4 million new service jobs in the Nine, many of them public sector 'non-market' ones. In the US during those years a total of 13 million new jobs were created, 11 million in the private sector and largely in services and the rest in the public sector too. That kept unemployment around 6 million until the late 1970s.

Had the industrial countries not suddenly slowed the productivity growth that had been such a feature of the 1960s, the effect on employment would have been catastrophic. One estimate has suggested that by 1978 the United States would have been facing joblessness totalling 14 million people if between 1973–7 its productivity growth rates had remained at 1960–73 levels. For Britain that figure would have been 3·6 million instead of 1·4 million unemployed by 1978, for West Germany 2·7 million, France, 2·5 million, Italy 5 million, against the 1 million or so at that time unemployed in each, while for Japan the productivity versus jobs trade-off was the most dramatic of them all. Had Japanese industry after the first oil 'shokko' stuck to its previous productivity levels, joblessness would have increased tenfold, reaching 12·6 million instead of the 1·3 million actually registered.[2]

Averting a jobs debacle on the scale those figures suggest was vital at any cost. In the seven leading industrial powers that attend the Western economic summits – the EEC's 'Big Four', Japan, Canada and the US – unemployment by 1978 could have been 42 million people rather than 13 million. If stagnant productivity was not a cheap price to pay, it was at any rate painless. But with the fourteen or so newly industrialized countries, the NICs such as South Korea or Brazil offering increasingly tough international competition, it is a currency that is almost used up, and an added worry is that a number of those jobs are still extremely vulnerable. Created by a 'sponge' of low productivity that mopped up unemployment, they risk being wrung out in a single savage twist.

The United States during those years from 1973 to the end of the decade was in fact trading a zero increase in productivity for all those jobs. As there are reckoned to be almost 2 million people in that sponge, they represent a readily accessible means for America to improve its productivity.[3] Even without that happening, US unemployment is again on a fast rising trend. The mid-1981 figure of over 7·75 million Americans registered as unemployed was at that time expected to be swelled to about 9 million people by the end of 1982, largely as a direct result of President Reagan's budget cuts. In October 1981, about 450,000 people, mainly from such underprivileged categories as black teenagers, were 'released' from the various federal schemes for training and work experience, while the AFL-CIO umbrella organization for the labour movement in the US believes that in all the cuts will mean 1·1 million more unemployed.[4] Forecasts of ten per cent or even twelve per cent unemployment in the US no longer seem very wild. Indeed, they look increasingly conservative, for by the end of 1981 registered US unemployment had climbed to 9·5 million, or 8·9 per cent, in defiance of all the experts.

Productivity, oddly enough, threatens Japan with mass unemployment too, although not in the classic sense that Japan has accustomed its competitors to. For Japan's problem is its rapidly aging workforce, and it provides an neat example of how productivity is not just a matter of cracking a whip to raise output. Wage costs are an equally essential factor in the equation, and, thanks to pay rates based on age seniority, companies like Matsushita will by 1990 be paying one-third more in wages than now.[5] Japanese industry's first reaction is its current reassessment of 'lifetime employment', meaning early retirement for many at around 50. That could put several million prime working-age men on the streets. How serious the aging phenomenon is can be gauged from the fact that at present each Japanese pensioner is supported by 15 workers, and by 2015 the burden will be shared by only three. Japan's jobs crisis is already taking shape. Visibly the number of jobless has risen to 1·3 million on a 54 million workforce and there are thought to be a further 4 million hidden unemployed. Then there are 4 million jobs in traditional industry expected to go and 10 million 'stone age' wholesale and retail jobs which streamlining and the micro-chip could cut through in swathes.[6]

The OECD estimates, that most member governments would rather not run through a computer and transform into an official projection, are being borne out by a variety of independent forecasts elsewhere. All agree that the jobs crisis, particularly in Europe, has in the early 1980s not even begun to show its true dimensions. Where they sometimes disagree is over whether the mid-1980s will see the nadir, or whether that will be in the 1990s instead. Put another way, few forecasters disagree that in most European countries 1984–6 will see the peaking of the 1960s baby boom and therefore the greatest human pressure on the market jobs; but some believe that the technological pressures of microelectronics in the following decade will be worse still. A middle view is that with any luck the baby boom and high technology problems will not greatly overlap, but that, once the demographic bulge is absorbed, micro-electronics will take over to sustain high rates of unemployment.

The European Commission in Brussels is now concerned that joblessness has become the single greatest political and economic challenge to the Community. Ivor Richard, the Social Affairs Commissioner who was formerly Britain's ambassador to the UN and before that a Labour MP, has warned that by the mid-1980s unemployment in the Ten could jump by a third again to top 12 million people. A number of the latest projections suggest that is unfortunately a highly conservative figure, and indeed Richard himself is increasingly of that view.

An exercise by the UN's International Labour Office in Geneva has lately projected alarming unemployment figures for West Germany, France and Holland, yet they are already being echoed by the jobless figures themselves. Although they are considerably higher than government organizations in those countries are themselves projecting, the ILO experts have pointed out that their new figures are in a way minimalist because they do not take into account unregistered jobless. They also based their computerized calculations on comparatively benign economic assumptions in all three countries throughout the 1980s.[7]

By 1990 they estimated that in West Germany the gap between labour force supply and demand will have widened to such an extent that unemployment in the Federal Republic will be over 2 million. In France it is forecast by the ILO study to reach 3·1 million in 1985 and to rise to 3·8 million by 1990. In the case of France, incidentally, it should be stressed that the policy assumptions made were Giscardian and pre-Mitterrand. It does, however, mean that the new French government has a projected 15 per cent registered unemployment rate to whittle away at. For Holland the 1990 jobless total is put at 840,000, giving a rate of 14·3 per cent. In August 1980 Dutch unemployment hit a postwar peak with a quarter of a million on the dole, and the country's Central Planning Office has indicated that by 1985 the figure will be half a million. In fact, it rose to 433,000 before 1981 was out. France's potential unemployment level is now openly recognized by a government which after all came to power on the back of those figures. In West Germany's case, there was for a while some doubt as to its vulnerability to the crisis. Although the ILO study had assumed 3·5 per cent economic growth when projecting its unemployment increases, other experts claimed that the same 3·5 per cent growth rate would help peg joblessness at around the 1 million-plus mark. In West Berlin, however, the German Institute for Economic Research had cautioned that, as the jobs problem began to make itself felt in the Federal Republic, registered unemployment would edge past 1·4 million as early as end-1981. In the event, they were way out as the figure was 1·7 million, and is still rising.

Those three EEC countries, needless to say, are among the most resilient of European economies. In others the jobs crisis is expected to strike considerably deeper. In Belgium, which already has the highest rate of registered unemployment of any EEC country, the total number of jobless could well double by 1985. In mid-1981 the collapse of traditional exporting industries, in a country that along with Britain had been a cradle of the industrial revolution, had put over 330,000 Belgians on the dole, giving a jobless rate that the EEC calculated at 10·5 per cent. There were warnings that by the mid-80s the total number of Belgians out of work could go to 450,000, or even 600,000, but by the end of that year they had been eclipsed by the official unemployment figures themselves, which had soared to 420,000.

Ireland vies neck-and-neck with Belgium for the doubtful honour of heading the EEC's unemployment league, and, with economic slowdown combining with birthrates traditionally higher than Italy's mezzogiorno, estimates of joblessness in the Irish Republic are beginning to defy calculation. There were in mid-1981 about 125,000 registered unemployed, giving an EEC rate of 10·3 per cent, and half of that total were under 25 years old. To keep joblessness down to that level Ireland needs during the 1980s over 26,000 new jobs every year, while the average number of new jobs created during the high-growth heyday of the 1970s was 10,000 a year. Registered unemployment of around twenty per cent, in a society that has moved dramatically off the land so that two-thirds of the population is now urban, looks increasingly inevitable.

Assessing the impact of the baby boom on Italy is an even more hazardous task. The figures suggest at least a million more jobseekers during the eighties who will be in search of work that does not apparently exist. But as a *Financial Times* correspondent reported plaintively from Rome even ten years ago: 'Italian statistics seem to come from fairyland. Those relating to the working population paint a glowing picture with little more than one-third of Italy's total population working or wanting to work. The other two-thirds are said to be made up of contented housewives, boys and girls attending school or doing their National Service, men and women of leisure and happy pensioners enjoying the sunshine.' He added that Italian Labour Ministry officials in fact reckoned that hidden unemployment totalled up to 2·5 million people then, which would have brought the real figure to about 3 million, while today that registered joblessness has increased by a factor of four to about 2 million. At a rough guess, and divining Italian unemployment rates can never be much more than that, the 1980s promise an apparent unemployment total of around 3 million and a real one nearer 5 million.

British economists, of course, do not make rough guesses. But their forecasts differ wildly.

At the bottom, and reassuring, end of the scale there are the claims of the Liverpool group of economists who have used a 'monetarist' econometric model to predict that UK unemployment will drop to 1·7 million by 1984 once the overall economy emerges leaner and fitter from recession. At the top end there is the Cambridge Economic Policy Group using a 'Keynesian' model that sees joblessness racing ahead to 4 million by 1984, and, without any allowance being made for the effects of microtechnology, sees it reaching 4·6 million by the end of the decade. There are also a number of estimates by trades union leaders that, although not based on the same elaborately scientific methods, are quite possibly no less valid for that. Clive Jenkins and his ASTMS union experts have predicted 5 million by 1983 and nearing the 4 million mark by the end of 1982 if jobs continue to disappear at the rate of 80,000 a month, while TUC leaders say that real UK unemployment was in any case over 3·5 million in mid-1981 and must continue to rise, although the rate of increase could be braked by a reverse in economic policy.[8]

The consensus lies in the middle ground, which looks safer than being at the extremes but may well not be. Many of its inhabitants have after all been proved wrong already. Their assumptions, that the jobs crisis instead of having a dynamic of its own merely entails modifications to conditions that their computer models can handle, have led to disastrous under-estimation of the problem. Former Employment Secretary Jim Prior admitted not long before being moved over to the Northern Ireland Office: 'The problem is now getting worse a good deal quicker than we anticipated'.[9] He added, true to the doctrine of ministerial responsibility, 'If that is a criticism of me, I accept it.' But it is much more a criticism of inaccurate professional forecasting. So, for what it is worth, the bulk of the forecasters see the unemployment snowball slowing in Britain but on no account falling very far. The most optimistic view is that of the London Business School experts who see it declining slightly to around 2·5 million by 1984 but who exclude school leavers even though they represent a major factor. Cambridge Econometrics, separate from CEPG, sees 3·5 million by 1985, stabilizing at 3·6 million until 1990 and then hitting 4 million by the mid-1990s. An unpublished Treasury forecast is alleged to target 3·7 million by 1983.

There is something to be said for the irreverent opinion that, judging by their track records, the forecasters would do well to look up from their calculations from time to time and glance out of the window. But it is in many ways an unkind criticism, for not only has the jobs crisis begun to create unfamiliar new conditions but also it is unclear exactly what is being measured. It looks simple enough if you believe that all that is required is to count the number of heads in a dole queue, but unfortunately the unemployed are a disconcertingly fluid population who defy simple arithmetic. Yet it is also crucial to do the calculations, for the nature of joblessness has changed – and greatly for the worse at that.

Time was, until not so long ago, that unemployment in the post-war era was something that even those afflicted suffered very briefly. In the mid-60s, before the British started improving the names of institutions rather than their performances, the Labour Exchanges were aptly titled. About half of all people who signed on were back in work within a fortnight. Ten years later that sort of frictional unemployment, where people were basically just between jobs, was still predominant. In the mid-1970s about half of all jobless left the register again inside a month and all but one person in ten were back in work within six months. In both those periods the figures of a fortnight and a month on the dole were calculated to be the median length of unemployment, and now in the early 1980s that median has increased dramatically to around four months.[10] These figures are important, because although it is sometimes said that, as 7 million people in Britain still change jobs yearly, unemployment therefore remains largely frictional, that is not the case. Those people who are on the register for less than thirteen weeks have a comparatively encouraging one-in-three chance of finding another job, while those on it for over a year see their chances dwindling to one-in-ten. A sediment of largely unemployable long term jobless is thus being formed very quickly. In early 1981 those out of work for over a year had risen to 430,000 and through a near geometric progression numbered 700,000 by late summer.[11] Those figures, it has also been pointed out, underrate long term joblessness because if a person is sick, which is frequently a concomitant of unemployment, he goes off the dole while on sickness benefit and on recovery starts the dole afresh.

Perhaps the best way of looking at unemployment, and therefore being able the better to measure it, is to liken it to one of those bathwater arithmetical problems so beloved of the authors of school textbooks. Water runs in from the tap at a given rate and out through the plug-hole at another, so how soon is the bath empty? Only this time on a hugely complicated basis, for there are many taps and many plug-holes and additional factors that have to be taken into consideration are the temperature of the water and because of the air temperature the rate of evaporation.

The taps pouring the unemployed into the bath are the following; school-leavers and university graduates, redundancy victims in manufacturing and services together with public sector victims of government spending cuts, women who had not held a job but who are now for whatever reason looking for part-time or even whole-time work, people whose time on one or other of the government's temporary schemes such as the Youth Opportunities Programme has expired, returning emigrants and expatriates, immigrants, illegal and otherwise, the recovered sick and so on. A number of these people may pass straight through the bath and down a plug-hole, therefore having no effect on the water level. Those are the people who although without a job never register for benefit. The TUC reckons that a quarter of all men who are really unemployed and 45 per cent of working women are unregistered, but that does not necessarily mean that they have never registered.

It is much more likely that they have at some point been into the bath but after varying lengths of time are drawn down the plug-hole marked 'discouraged'. Unable to get a job they withdraw from the labour market and so reduce the level of the bathwater that is the volume of registered unemployment. Often discouragement prevents people from even going into the bath. Young people, above all in countries where families are very supportive so that girls, in particular, stay at home when there are no jobs about, evaporate off the apparent joblessness totals as soon as they leave the 'tap'.

The various plug-holes down which the bathwater of unemployment can go are fairly obvious. One is marked employment, another government schemes that frequently consist of 'make-work' projects; still another is emigration while there are also training and further education plug-holes. The two labelled 'discouraged' and 'unregistered' are confusingly close together.

But what determines the depth of the bathwater is of course not only the number but also the diameter of the plug-holes.

The employment plug-hole has been shrinking fast of late, especially for skilled engineering jobs in manufacturing industry where the ratio between the number of unemployed and the number of available job openings has gone from 2:1 in mid-1979 to 25:1 at the end of 1980 and is still widening. Throughout 1980, though, the various jobs holes remained surprisingly wide and were taking a constant 270,000 people a month off the dole in Britain. The major problem was that the tap had been opened further and was pouring the registered jobless into the bath at a monthly rate that went from 276,000 in early 1979 to 370,000 by the end of 1980. Enlarging all the other plug-holes at the bottom naturally helps reduce the volume of bathwater, but is not a sure-fire solution.[12]

It might help explain the nature of the problem if, instead of pouring water, the various unemployment taps were considered to be releasing different liquids, each with particular characteristics and viscosities. There are a variety of youth taps, ranging from deprived and potentially violent male teenagers to those with an industrial background who are being denied apprenticeships, to women clerical workers menaced by the micro-chip, right up to hard-to-place graduates. They are none of them really susceptible to just a single plug-hole marked employment, each of the liquids is drawn to different ones. Unskilled, uneducated youth is the least likely to escape down any plughole, of course, save that marked 'discouraged'. But the qualified are also increasingly being denied the chance to leave unless they take jobs well below their capabilities.

The problem of youth unemployment has assumed alarming proportions throughout Europe and North America of late. On the principle of 'last come, last served', young people find it hard to elbow their way into an extremely tight labour market. In fact they do, of course, but, as there are increasingly fewer 'natural' openings for them, further complications are raised by the fact that they displace older and less adequate workers. As it

is, if job openings for youth remain at the same level as today –
which in labour market terms is a rather optimistic assumption –
there are fears that, as the EEC's baby boom gets into its stride
in the mid-80s, nearly half of the Community's total unemployed
could consist of under 28-year olds with little real work experience.

In Britain, teenage unemployment is growing at three times
the national rate, and already almost 40 per cent of all unemployed are under-25s. So far the school-leavers' impact on the
UK jobless totals has been damped down statistically and cos-
metically. But, unless the schemes operated by the Manpower
Services Commission are greatly expanded and extended to
retain people on their strength, youth unemployment will rapidly
reach almost unmanageable levels. In mid-1981 the MSC was
privately warning the government that by 1983 teenagers on the
dole will have increased from less than 100,000 to an undisguis-
able 700,000. The situation is roughly the same elsewhere in
Europe. In West Germany just over twenty per cent of unemployment is made up of under-25s, but the crest of the Federal
Republic's baby boom wave is a few years behind that of Britain,
where the influx of young job seekers is just about peaking.
Germany's is just beginning and will last throughout the 1980s.
In France the under-25s account for 40 per cent of registered
unemployed, and in Italy it is close to 50 per cent.[13] For the
OECD as a whole, youth unemployment was triggering anxiety
back in 1977, when joblessness among young people was at ten
per cent and totalled 7 million. Official concern produced few
concrete results, though, and now that percentage has risen to
thirteen per cent.

Only one school-leaver in two was able to get a job in Britain
during 1981, and for 1982 that rough average dropped to one in
three. The danger of the jobs crisis producing a disaffected
generation is clear enough. Less easy to spot is the effect on
skilled workers. While they tend to find work again much more
easily than an unskilled manual labourer, they too are finding the
craft employment plug-hole increasingly narrow. Although they

represent a major asset to industry they now occupy a fast growing proportion of total unemployment. And like all unemployed, the longer they are out of a job the less likely they are to return to work.

The influence of women on the workings of the labour market is possibly the most difficult to analyse of all. Drawn to work by their millions in the 1960s and 1970s, they have been among the first to be rejected. On paper they account for about 45 per cent of all European unemployment, and in the UK around a third. Which suggests that they suffer no more than their fair share and sometimes less. But the paper figures of registered unemployed are misleading. Such are the waning attractions of ending up or remaining in the bathtub of the registered jobless, that the outflow into unregistered unemployment is accelerating. It is an established mechanism of labour markets that when pressure on jobs becomes really intense the rate at which people 'participate' in the market drops sharply. They are either discouraged from entering it or opt to leave it, and so do not show up on the books. The Germans call these unregistered potential workers the 'silent reserve', which at least has a positive ring to it, and in most European countries the invisible jobless are reckoned to represent a further twenty per cent that can be tacked on to the end of the registered unemployment figures. In France the figure is thought to be as high as one-third. The US Department of Labor has tried, since 1970, to measure the discouraged workforce, and said at the end of 1981 that it had reached a record 1·2 million people.

It sounds, at first, like a useful safety valve. Those who are not in serious need of work withdraw from the competition, no longer draw any benefit and reduce the politically troublesome unemployment figures. In reality, they make coping with the jobs crisis more difficult still.

It is true enough that the discouraged and the hidden unemployed in general are on the whole less desperate for work than those who stay on the register. But they do not obligingly stay out of the labour market if work should present itself. The French have found that for each 100 new jobs created in service industries only eighteen of the openings are filled by people who had been on the dole. The remaining 82 came in from outside the labour market.[14] It is a phenomenon that is the despair of job creation agencies and politicians; work is provided, often at great public expense, and scarcely a dent is made in the jobless totals. An indication of how seriously governments now take the disruptive capacity of the discouraged can be gleaned from the interest that a Danish project has aroused. Denmark's encouragement of early retirement to make more room in the labour market has been described as 'one of the great success stories' of job creation. Not because it is claimed to have reduced unemployment by two full percentage points, but because only a quarter of the new openings became occupied by the discouraged so that the rest came off the dole queues.

One conclusion that can reasonably be drawn from all this is that not only are registered unemployment figures more and more misleading as times get harder, they are also liable to be irrelevant. Taking a monthly 'snapshot' of the number of people who have signed on to the unemployment register is no doubt the only practical way of measuring joblessness, but it also happens to be a politically attractive method of under-playing its seriousness.

Take Britain in early 1981. Registered unemployment stood at 2·32 million people. But it can be roughly calculated that real unemployment was more like 3·75 million. For, over and above the registered total, the following elements can be added in: according to the government's survey of the General Household Register in early 1981, there were at that time up to 350,000 people, chiefly women, who could be considered as unregistered unemployed. There were also almost 250,000 unregistered teenagers who had left school but were still in statistical limbo. Discouraged workers were put at half a million and the MSC had about 340,000 people contained in its various schemes.

Add them all up and the total level of British unemployment was then a shade over 3·75 million even though there was intense speculation at the time as to whether joblessness would reach 2·5 million, let alone 3 million or more during 1981. More likely, though, there is some overlap between those sets of figures, so that some unregistered school-leavers show up in the household survey and some people in the household survey are included in the overall total of discouraged workers. A calculation in the *New Statesman* in March 1981, based on figures supplied by a Market & Opinion Research International poll, reckoned that the then 2·5 million 'headline' unemployment figure should really be 3·5 million. More important than guessing at the overlap, though, is the need to assess the cumulative nature of hidden unemployment. The half-million discouraged workforce has most of it grown up in the past eighteen months, while unregistered school-leavers are known to be increasing almost rhythmically—250,000 in early 1981, 350,000 in late 1981, 400,000 in early 1982 and so on. The pool of discouraged workers in Britain is estimated to be growing at about 150,000 people a year, so, even on the most conservative of estimates, 3 million registered jobless means at least 4 million people who would work if they could.

Some analysts have become rather impatient with all the imponderables that close scrutiny of the labour market throws up. They tend to prefer the blunter but more illuminating method of the jobs gap curve. It is a rather crude shorthand way of grossing up the difference between supply and demand, but has the effect of bringing the shortage of jobs into sharp focus. To get back to full employment, say Europe's trades unions, meaning the two per cent jobless level that was for long the post-war norm, about 11 million new jobs would be needed by 1985 in the EEC alone, and 15 million in Western Europe as a whole. In early 1980, after joblessness in the European Community had been steady for two years at around the six per cent mark, it was reckoned that to keep it down to that level in the coming five years would require 4 million net new jobs.

When the OECD experts arrived at their forecast of 35 million unemployed by the mid-1980s, it was being emphasized that by that stage figures become almost meaningless because of the discouragement factor. Indeed, by taking the various projections for just the leading OECD nations mentioned in this chapter, and adjusting them by an additional 20–30 per cent to take account for known discouragement levels, the total reached is around 35 million. It is not a wonderfully scientific method of confirming what was no doubt calculated in a much more detailed way. But one begins to wonder what *is* scientific in the welter of contradictory and overlapping pieces of information that go towards making up labour market statistics. As Peter Drucker, a foremost American expert, remarked in the *Wall Street Journal* a few years back: 'The last figure to look at is the one the newspapers print first; the official unemployment figure. Statistically it is an abomination, an Alice in Wonderland stew of apples, oranges and red herrings.'

What some OECD analysts wish they had, and technically it should be possible, is an econometric model so flexible and sophisticated that it would help forecast the two underlying factors that have already proved the downfall of almost all projections made so far – the collapse of manufacturing industry and the rise of micro-technological equipment that is becoming so cheap that it is beginning to make a nonsense of the traditional dilemma of capital intensive versus labour intensive investment. For thanks both to the micro-chip and to the decline of traditional manufacturing, literally hundreds of millions of jobs will hang in the balance.

3

The Disintegrating
Industrial Jalopy

The collapse of manufacturing industry in the world's wealthiest
countries is not unlike a silent movie. Hardly a stirring Valentino
melodrama but rather a Mack Sennett epic car chase at the end of
which a battered Model-T Ford slowly disintegrates.

At first, almost unnoticed, a single wheel drops away and
wobbles off ahead of the car. A look of disbelief and then
consternation as the errant wheel catches the driver's eye, followed by hysterical gesticulation as the car veers out of control
back and forth across the road before settling majestically into
the dust. The doors sag open, the steering wheel pops out and the
engine yields up a despairing cloud of steam before toppling
slowly forward off its mountings.

For the industrial nations of Europe, that first wheel became
detached almost twenty years ago, although its departure was
observed at the time with an almost monumental indifference.
For the early 1960s were the watershed at which the post-war
boom in manufacturing jobs shifted quite sharply away into an
expansion of non-manufacturing service jobs. From banks to
launderettes and advertising agencies to boutiques, it was the
activities that served the factories that began to provide the most
employment. By the end of the decade Europeans were stepping
into 1 million of these new service jobs every year. Against those,
only 100,000 new manufacturing jobs were being created
annually, and then chiefly by such heavily agricultural
but developing countries as Ireland, Spain, Portugal and
Greece.[1]

The next stage in the disintegration came with the Yom Kippur Arab-Israeli war in October 1973 and the ensuing first oil price shock. Deprived of their subsidy of cheap energy the industrial economies zig-zagged almost to a halt. But they soon decided the trouble was just a temporary fault, a cyclical hitch, and huge basic manufacturing industries like steel pressed ahead with new plant investment to be ready for the good times that the 1980s would bring.

Now that the 1980s are here, the jalopy is collapsing on to the road and bits are flying off in dramatic fashion. But the disintegration is far from over, for the manufacturing limousine that has given the wealthy Western countries such a smooth ride since the war still represents almost 100 million jobs. And they most of them now have only a one in two chance of survival.

How quickly those 100 million or so jobs become exposed to the danger of extinction is still very much a matter of conjecture. Some British analysts expect to see most of the really savage cuts in the UK manufacturing workforce of almost 7 million people taking place in a mega-crisis of the early 1980s, others elsewhere in Europe believe the debacle can be smoothed out over the decade. In the US there is a school of thought that the country's vertiginous drop from over 20 million manual manufacturing jobs to as few as 7 million will last for about 25 years.

Nobody knows, of course, even though the reasons for supposing the accelerating disappearance of manufacturing jobs in the industrialized countries are plain enough to be generally agreed on. So far, though, all that most forecasters have in common is that they have consistently underestimated the breathtaking speed of the collapse triggered by the 1980–1 onset of recession. To the most deeply distressed industries, such as steel, textiles, shipbuilding, automobile construction and engineering, listening to some short term forecasts must have been like hearing the weatherman promise one last fine day when outside it had already begun to rain.

For the rich countries' structure of inter-connecting industries that until recently had such a logical appearance – steel and engineering for years sustained each other in almost ecological balance – has instead turned out more like a house of cards. Shipbuilding's troubles send shockwaves into areas quite remote from one another, like heavy engineering and micro-electronics, and motor industry problems have an instant impact on textiles and petro-chemicals.

By late 1981, as shake-out gave way to shambles, the British experience had become a vivid example to other industrial countries of how quickly the ripple of depressed demand could spread across a sophisticated manufacturing economy. The Thatcher government's deflationary zeal was widely thought to have aggravated matters by denying companies of borderline viability the finance that might have enabled them to pull through, but in all too many cases the recession was placing intolerable strains on areas where UK manufacturing had become weak and vulnerable.

If there remained a nook or cranny of the British industrial landscape untouched by downturn and redundancy it was not evident. In the traditional base industries the mayhem was such that output sank to depths unplumbed since the Great Depression 50 years earlier. Approaching three-quarters of a million jobs in manufacturing industry disappeared as output dropped fourteen per cent. In the heartland of the engineering industry, the West Midlands, the number of people employed by companies grouped in the region's engineering employers' association fell in 1980 by a third. That core of 120,000 skilled jobs gone meant many more, while short-time working in the area became so prevalent that the West Midlands accounted for 40 per cent of all UK short-time. It was not for nothing that the area was soon labelled the Bermuda Triangle of British Industry.

Heavy casualties in engineering were to be expected, not least because of the waning fortunes of the motor industry. But the range of other manufacturing jobs that proved easy prey to recession was often an unpleasant surprise. At both ends of the industrial spectrum – high technology across to traditional crafts – manufacturing became a risky occupation. Lay-offs at

Wedgwood seemed to go almost hand-in-hand with massive redundancies at ICL, the UK's flagcarrier computer and electronics producer where the end of 1980 saw the workforce trimmed by 2000 people down to 7000. And throughout the audio industry half of all employees went on to short-time as imports surged to take a full three-quarters of the British market.

In soft consumer goods sectors, jobs also evaporated. Powerful breweries such as Allied and Whitbread announced lay-offs, as did tobacco majors like Imperial, Gallaher, Carreras and John Player. Confectionery, soap and toiletries, pharmaceuticals and luxury goods all suffered along with the makers of consumer durables and white goods. There were, too, some unlikely victims such as workers in the normally recession-proof malt whisky distilleries of Scotland and the Norwich plant that cut back on the 40 million Christmas crackers it usually produces. Luggage-makers and suppliers of school uniforms, printers and research chemists, potters and bottle-makers all joined the dole queues. And as the economic machine lost momentum, the providers of key services and utilities suffered in their turn. Dockers around Britain's ports were declared redundant and the Central Electricity Generating Board found itself forced to scrap its own oil saving plan by mothballing a score of coal burning power stations.

But it was the speed and ferocity with which the recession gnawed at the hard industrial core of the manufacturing base that began to provoke the greatest concern, for many of those job losses implied an irreversible contraction of the country's industrial muscle. Manufacturing industry slimmed down and re-equipped with new technology in order to fight back in international markets was one thing, for its profits can sustain service industries that provide new employment. But manufacturing industry starved to death, it rapidly became clear, was quite another proposition.

With the early 1981 closure of the French-owned Talbot car plant at Linwood, attention centred on the drive-shaft importance of Britain's ailing motor industry. If Linwood was any microcosm, the consequences of further decline let alone collapse would be catastrophic. The loss of 4500 car-making jobs there helped push overall unemployment in the area to 40 per cent, adding what one observer wryly termed another exhibit to the 'museum belt' of empty factories in west central Scotland.

Britain's motor manufacturers now produce about half as many cars as ten years ago, when yearly output was around 1·7 million units. Yet the motor industry remains the largest single generator of skilled jobs in the country. BL, as stricken British Leyland prefers to call itself, directly employs only 160,000 people or so, but calculations of how many other engineering and supplier industry jobs are directly linked range from a BL management one that the company provides 600,000 people with employment to a trade union claim that the true jobs total around BL is 1 million.[2] In any event, the company farms out around half a billion pounds in sub-contracted work every year and many of the UK's largest engineering groups are heavily reliant on BL. Lucas, Dunlop and Guest, Keen & Nettlefold (GKN), each with sales turnovers of more than £1 billion a year, between them rely for an average fifteen per cent of their business on BL. Other companies like Rubery Owen, Automotive Products and Rockwell are even more dependent, with twenty per cent of their sales tied to BL.[3]

The importance of the motor industry can be judged by further estimates, such as the suggestion that in engineering centres such as Birmingham 300,000 jobs – one in four – would disappear if motor manufacturing went under. Unfortunately, in Britain as elsewhere in Europe, the prognosis of the industry's future health is far from encouraging. BL is due to shed up to 24,000 jobs by the end of 1982, while Ford UK aims to cut back by 25,000 jobs to achieve a 40 per cent reduction in its workforce by 1985. And the export markets that have been a lifeline to Britain's components producers are also shrinking for them. In the mid-1970s, the UK's overseas sales of components were twice the value of imported ones, but by 1980 those exports worth £2 billion were only 50 per cent greater than imports. Some forecasters are now suggesting that, thanks in large part to pressure from Japan, the number of component-producing companies throughout Europe will by 1990 have shrunk by a third.

Looking at the shifts and contractions of the industries of the world's rich countries is, however, a bit like being a seismologist. It helps to have the perspective of time when establishing whether a pattern of quakes exists. The first tremors to shake the manufacturing supremacy of the US and the Western European nations could be recorded in the early 1960s, and by the middle sixties could be plainly felt through the soles of the feet. The developed countries were at that time 'either negligent or, worse still, wilfully indifferent in their response to the signs of trouble', Santosh Mukherjee, an economic expert at the UN's International Labour Office, later noted.[4] The industrialized countries were by then on the slippery slope, for although between 1964 and 1973 the employment provided by manufacturing dropped only by four per cent, between 1973 and 1976 that trend started to accelerate sharply with a two per cent further drop each year.[5] By 1978 it had picked up more speed still, so that during the five years from 1973 the EEC countries alone lost 3 million industrial jobs, reducing their collective manufacturing workforce to 40 million people.[6]

But rather like the squiggles on a seismographic monitor that can be meaningless or downright misleading unless set against a wider context of Richter Scale activity over the years, a number of factors obscured the trend and prevented it from being easily recognizable. The boom-before-the-bust year of 1973, when most of the leading industries hit a peak at which they were producing one and a half times to twice as much as ten years before, helped to condition thinking that the 1974–5 recession was just a temporary hiccup. Anyway, at that time it was really only Europe that was losing its manufacturing jobs. In the US the manufacturing sector in 1973 employed twenty-one per cent more people than in 1960. Japan, needless to say, was also romping ahead with year-on-year increases in the size of manufacturing industry. In 1973 it had overtaken America, where about 29 per cent of the workforce was then in manufacturing and had 36 per cent of its workers productively busy in the new factories.

At the time, it was said that there was only one skilled Japanese worker for every two available jobs. Yet by the following year both Japan and the US had joined the Europeans in experiencing a slide not just in manufacturing jobs as a whole but in entire industrial sectors that now threaten to disappear.

The Japanese, in contrast to their popular image of being one of the prime causes of the world's economic woes, have suffered too. The 1970s produced serious falls in Japan's output of basic manufactured goods like steel, chemicals, non-ferrous metals, lumber and, most of all, in textiles. Manufacturing employment went into reverse and declined from almost 14·5 million people to around 13 million, and projections by the Tokyo government have suggested that by the late 1980s it will have dwindled to only 10 million jobs out of a total workforce that will have gone from about 54 million now up to 60 million.[7]

In the US, the flight from manufacturing industry has also been pronounced. By the end of the 1970s it was providing work for only one American in five, and that shrinkage would probably have been greater had there not been heavy emphasis on finding work for almost 20 million young Americans, the fruits of the 1950s baby bulge, who during the decade swelled the US labour force by 25 per cent. That almost unconscious acceptance of job-sharing yielded very noticeable falls in US productivity rates, while a secondary phenomenon was the mood among American employers that it was safer and cheaper to put people into their factories than new machines. People, after all, could be 'let go'.

And let go they were. By late 1980 it had become clear that America's attempts to slow the leakage of manufacturing jobs that had begun in 1973 had in fact so eroded its ability to withstand really tough international competition. The blood-letting of the second oil price-triggered recession turned quickly into an unstoppable haemorrhage.

One million jobs in American manufacturing disappeared early on, with there being plainly no hope of them being re-established even after the recession. By the autumn of that year, there were over 2 million unemployed in heavy industry and engineering, and a further 1·25 million-plus out of work in construction, transport and the utilities. The country's jobless blue-collar workers numbered 4 million, or half of the total unemployed. In Detroit a quarter of the automobile industry's workforce was laid off in a brutal wave of sackings that revived memories of the 1930s, and the city's mayor, Coleman Young, warned that the Detroit industry's survival also meant the survival of a further 16 million jobs elsewhere in the US – almost a sixth of the entire workforce.[8]

Most American experts now agree that the whittling away of the manufacturing sector's importance as a provider of employment is inevitable. Eli Ginzberg, a Columbia University economist in New York who is a Grand Old Man in the business of analysing employment trends, reckons that by 1995 only fifteen per cent of all jobs will be in manufacturing. Peter Drucker, the US management expert, sees the run down going even further, if not necessarily faster. He puts manufacturing work in turn of the century America at between 12 million and 7 million people. Neither forecaster is particularly concerned by such developments, for both assume that such developments would result from a highly efficient and technological industry whose very profitable added value goods would be able to support an enormous service sector. Drucker recently likened the future of US industry to the recent past of American agriculture. There, he points out, employment has since World War II dropped from 30 per cent of the entire labour force to just five per cent, while farm output has just about tripled. Futuristically, he sees the use of micro-processor automation, low-entropy flow processes based on membrane-reverse-osmosis and genetically manipulated micro-organisms as neatly compatible with the growth of a highly educated US industrial workforce.[9]

This vision of a few white-coated technicians producing goods that are so superior and profitable that 80–90 per cent of the population can be supported by them is attractive and quite widespread. It also is beginning to look suspiciously like an economist's 'assumption' that because industrialized countries have been losing manufacturing jobs, and because productivity increases in which fewer of their highly paid workers produce more are vital if they are to remain competitive, this de-industrialization process can continue almost indefinitely. But it is an assumption that needs looking at very closely indeed.

Service jobs are just that, services to manufacturing industry. They depend on both the value and the volume of the goods being churned out by the factories. As there are really very few 'new' goods being invented, merely new machines for making old goods or such improvements on old goods as electric coffee mills that displaced manual grinders, the industrial countries have to think carefully about which products they will continue to make.

Those two respected American economists both seem in danger of glibness when they explain how the US manufacturing sector will become so much more compact. Drucker has suggested that the more low grade manufacturing processes can simply be transferred to the developing world,[10] while Ginzberg points out that New York City is already 'an 85 per cent service economy' and adds that all economies in any case depend not on the production of goods 'but the taking in of each other's washing'.

Both viewpoints of course contain a large element of truth but if taken at face value risk promoting a dangerous sense of complacency. Much the same can be said of economic forecasters now scanning the horizons of the 1990s who predict sharp falls in manufacturing employment and then assume that those job losses will be made good by employment in services and government.

If those who view the contraction of manufacturing employment with something akin to equanimity have in mind fewer people producing much the same goods as now, in much the same amounts, their lack of panic is understandable; although it still leaves unsolved the problem of how the same level of goods supports an even larger number of unproductive people without there being a proportionate drop in standards of living. But much more important is the fact that producing the same types of goods as now, and in the same amounts, is no longer available as an option for the industrialized countries.

Whole industries are going, and the really worrying thing is that on the whole they are 'generative' industries that create work and wealth in a plethora of mini-industries. They are also enormous employers of labour in their own right. Europe's 'sick' industries – steel, textiles, cars and shipbuilding – are reckoned to account for a stunning 40 per cent of the EEC's manufacturing jobs. Yet for all of them the writing is already on the wall to some degree or other.

Six million jobs in the EEC depend directly on motor car manufacturing. Yet in countries like Spain, where cheaper labour is attracting some of the biggest new plant investments, there is already an awareness that the industry may well be just passing through. The joke in Madrid goes that as motor manufacturing drifts south from Coventry and even Wolfsburg, through France and now into Spain, it will eventually settle somewhere close to the equator. Maybe Mauretania, the Madrilenos sourly jest.

Beside the other ailing industries, motor manufacturing is the least vulnerable. For both Europe and the US the chances of retaining steel industries on anything like the same scale as now seem remote. Europe's textile industry, which has been estimated to provide the livelihood of one European in seven, faces decimation in the foreseeable future. And for shipbuilding, one of the greatest generative industries of all, the irreversible process of collapse has long begun.

Experts who have been trying to peer into the uncertain future of the motor industry have suggested that by 1990 the sector will have been so dramatically slimmed down that only eight different manufacturers will be left in the world.[12] The argument is that the economies of scale required by a manufacturer to remain competitive will mean a minimum yearly output of 2 million cars. The industry is therefore due to be shaken by a series of closures, rationalizations and mergers, and for Europe the prediction is that only four companies will survive – Volkswagen, Fiat, Renault and Peugeot-Citroen. How true that turns out to be remains to be seen, although forecasting future trends in the car industry seems a thankless task with all too many predictions turning out very wide of the mark.

In 1978, for instance, the analysts went on the record with estimates that the 1977 record of 10 million cars sold in Europe promised a boom in which the EEC market would take over 12 million cars a year by the early 1980s.[13] In 1979 the manufacturers did indeed lift sales in the EEC to 10·4 million units, but that was also the year of OPEC's staccato of oil shocks that lifted oil prices overall by 150 per cent. In 1980 the bottom almost fell out of the car market and sales in the EEC plummeted to 8·4 million. Various sales levels for the years up to 1985 are now being forecast, ranging from a high of 11·25 million to a much lower 9·6 million,[14] but the magic figure of 12 million has been put back somewhat arbitrarily to 1990.[15] In the valuable commercial vehicles market, the forecasters do not see sales in Europe climbing back to the 1980 level of just over 1 million units until 1984.[16]

The signs are, though, that for the European industry the challenge will be not so much one of returning to the golden days of the 1970s as of hanging on like grim death to its already much eroded market share. Productivity will be the deciding factor, and that implies heavy job shedding.

Europe's car producers take about a fifth of Europe's steel, but it is not really the ups and downs of the motor manufacturers that have produced chaos and closure in steel. For the giant steel industry, mainspring of industrial progress and wealth, is beginning to look like an inoperable case. Almost half of European steel production plants now lie idle, transformed overnight, it sometimes seems, from being the rocket launchers of economic take-off to the dinosaurs of a passing industrial age.

As with the motor industry, the 1980s have so far been terrible years for steel. Yet the start of the decade had not long before been forecast as the point at which the industry could expect to enter a new and golden era. In the early 1970s, when crucial investment decisions were being taken, it was confidently believed that the early eighties would see European steel consumption at such a high level that production would top 200 million tonnes a year, almost double present levels. The problem, as the planners saw it, was to ensure that Europe's steelmakers could meet that demand in order to prevent imported steel being sucked in. It was not shortsightedness on the part of steel industry managers, quite the opposite. It was sound decision making in an industry grown arrogant on a post-war growth record that had consistently outstripped all other sectors. The real problem since has been not merely that consumption stumbled in the 1974–5 recession and then fell hard in 1980, but that steel industry managements cannot believe they are suffering more than a temporary reverse. Their management thinking, despite the fact that in the EEC alone steel jobs have dropped from 800,000 to 600,000 since 1974, is that steel's difficulties are cyclical rather than structural. They find it hard to rid themselves of the belief that at some future date steel will once again be profitable business.

The more hard-headed view is that, as a major employer, steel now faces two options, and between them they add up to a no-win situation.

Either the steelmakers must cut back savagely on their overcapacity, which means a round of plant closures and lay-offs on a scale hitherto unimagined, or the market will do it for them. By 1985 the European governments are due to stop paying their steelmakers the subsidies that enable them to stay in business. Without that financial safety net most of Europe's major steel producers would collapse under the weight of operating losses that now total almost $3 billion a year. The more likely alternative, though, is determined restructuring to close the gap between capacity and real output. At present, Europe's steelworks are capable of producing over 200 million tonnes of steel a year, but are working at only about 55 per cent of their capacity. The job shedding involved in narrowing that gap to a point where 85 per cent of capacity is in use could add up to almost a quarter of a million steelworker redundancies still to come.

Because steel jobs are highly concentrated in steel towns, the industry has a very strong political profile. Yet arguably it does not represent such a serious employment problem as do other failing sectors. Shipyards are also a focus of sudden and sweeping redundancies, but their real importance is the business they provide for a wide range of other industries. Shipbuilding is akin to assembling a huge industrial jig-saw puzzle; inside a ship's casing of steel the products of thousands of supplier companies are fitted intricately together. In the heyday of shipbuilding, when the great transatlantic liners vied against each other to secure the Blue Riband for the fastest crossing, the shipyards themselves manufactured an enormous variety of products. At Harland & Wolff's Belfast yard, where the *Titanic* was built, there was once a studio with north light where a row of artists painted the canvases that would hang in the liners' staterooms. Now something like 70 per cent of a ship's price tag is bought in through sub-contracts, and shipping's illness is highly infectious for the rest of manufacturing industry.

Shipbuilding has already taken hard knocks in the years since 1975. Shipyard jobs in the EEC have been reduced by 42 per cent and now stand at 115,000, but the pressures for further cutbacks are intense. The European governments are between them reckoned to be spending half a billion pounds a year in subsidies – a fifth of the value of each vessel built – to hold the line against fierce competition from South East Asia and East European yards. In the US the picture is even bleaker, for at no reasonable level of subsidies are American shipyards capable of competing for international business, while the industry's domestic order books have shrunk from 5 million tonnes in 1974 to just over 1 million in 1981.

By 1978 the situation was thought so bad in the EEC that the

European Commission was urging a 35 per cent cutback in ship-yard capacity that would have entailed the loss of 75,000 jobs. It is currently advocating a rather less drastic trimming, because of stern resistance on the part of governments to the axing of a strategically important industry, so that 25,000 shipyard jobs are being targeted. Britain and Italy have both been singled out as the two EEC countries that should bear the brunt of this restruc-turing, with the UK being told by Brussels that it must greatly improve its productivity, and so reduce the labour force, and Italy being urged to close yards. Hanging on to the sophisticated high technology end of the world shipping market, such as liquid gas carriers, has now become Europe's chief priority. For Britain, it is to safeguard its position as Western Europe's largest warships' producer, ranking only behind the US and the Soviet Union.

For each shipyard job there are three others directly linked to it and still more that rely indirectly on orders from shipbuilders. However, shipbuilding's difficulties are in simple job terms almost as nothing beside the troubles of textiles.

The story is much the same as in so many other industries. Either textiles and clothing producers streamline themselves into internationally competitive shape, which could involve sacking one worker in two in the interests of improving productivity, or they lose much the same number of jobs willy-nilly to interna-tional competition. The difference between the textiles sector and most others is the sheer size of the threatened industry.

In the European Community there are thought to be about 4 million people employed in producing textiles and garments. The exact number is hard to establish because of the large fringe of casual labour that surrounds the sector, from cottage indus-tries to barely legal sweatshops in inner-cities and even Indonesians in offshore, anchored ships, allegedly to be found off the Dutch coast. In Italy alone, there are estimated to be half a million outworkers. Textiles is also one of the most oddly heterogeneous industries, for at its uppermost end it encom-passes the sophisticated man-made fibres industry, that accounts in Europe for a quarter of all petro-chemicals consumption, and in its lower reaches it includes a flotsam of fly-by-night operators.

The inroads into the European industry that have already been carved by international competition have also affected these widely different businesses quite even-handedly. The textile industry's labour force is now about 1 million people less than it was ten years ago, and of late the UK's man-made fibre industry has been cut by half. Some of the trouble comes from the Third World, whose low-priced textile products can be unbeatably priced, but a good deal also comes from the giant textile factories of the US and of Eastern Europe. Carpets and curtains or sheets and suitings are nowadays produced by the mile in these new super-efficient complexes, while European factories still measure by the metre. The EEC has more than 30,000 textile-related companies, but it has been said that the problem is no longer how to save the textile industry but what to save of it. At the bottom line it looks as if 2 million more manufacturing jobs must go there during the 1980s.

Running through most of these horror stories of coming industrial decline and fall there is a common thread. Biggest is best. Car producers must be able to turn out at least 2 million vehicles a year, single integrated steel complexes are the only form of steelmaking efficient enough to survive, textile mills must clock up daily mileage not yardage. The investment costs in industries already desperately unprofitable will be colossal, and the immediate return on the cash outlay can only be greater unemployment.

But to confuse matters there is an unsettling counterpoint to this theme. An increasingly large body of opinion has it that there are many manufacturing industries where in the near future small will not merely be beautiful but the only way to remain viable. The downsizers argue that some of the great industrial combines, the victors in the last Thirty Years War of takeover battles, may now be mammoths facing sudden extinction. Eli Ginzberg in the US argues cogently that the new micro-electronic technology, thanks to its rapidly reducing price tag, could be the great leveller that will permit small industrial operations to be as efficient as large ones. Sweden's Academy of Engineering Sciences has gone one better and warned that large companies are too 'bureaucratic and clumsy' to handle new technology projects as effectively as their smaller competitors. But that effectiveness means, of course, the ability to marshal fewer people and more machines faster.[17]

Whether medium sized and small companies will start to buck the trend is not, however, of immediate relevance. Much more urgent is the future of the largely state-owned lame ducks of industry that are both giant employers and strategically vital to each country's national security. For one of the most powerful reasons for maintaining, for instance, steel production in a world in which the steel glut will probably not be eradicated before the end of this century is the military impotence that depending on overseas suppliers would entail.

Motor manufacturing, shipbuilding, chemicals, petro-chemicals, conventional and nuclear engineering are all no less crucial to the leading industrial countries' arms lockers. Their governments' views on the strictly economic advantages of pouring funds into the lengthening list of lame duck enterprises might be shaken, though, by the findings of another recent study commissioned by the Swedish government. The Swedish Industrial Economic Research Institute was asked to analyse the effects of public subsidies on what is, after all, still one of the very wealthiest industrial economies in the world, and came up with some disquieting conclusions. It found that the subsidies totalling almost £8 billion that during the past decade have made Swedish industry one of the most buttressed anywhere are in the longer term actually reducing employment. It is a controversial conclusion because Sweden's open-handed public spending policies and its two per cent registered unemployment rate have long been pointed to by trade unions elsewhere as a model for their own governments. The Swedish research analysts nevertheless concluded after looking at the steel, shipbuilding, timber and textiles industries that while in the short term demand was stimulated and jobs saved, in the longer term wage levels were pushed up so that unsubsidised companies were prevented from expanding. They calculated that by accepting an unemployment rate of 3–4 per cent and industrial output that would be 4–5 per cent lower, the country would after five years have forged ahead into a ten year period of expansion during which unemployment would be even lower than at present and output up to seven per cent higher.

Il faut reculer pour mieux sauter. There can be few policymakers who at heart still doubt that. But how to tell the workers and voters who will either become unemployed or will see their standards of living reduced? And how, too, to prevent cutback accelerating into collapse? Making manufacturing industry strong again is for all that vital, for there is no evidence to suggest that the industrialized countries grew rich on anything other than industry. Quite the contrary.

The New York Stock Exchange has devised a simple but effective formula for measuring countries' wealth, which it dubbed 'Economic Performance Indicator', or EPI. It is arrived at by calculating the ratio between real GDP growth and the combined unemployment and inflation rates, and multiplying that by 100. It shows clearly how the Western nations' years of manufacturing growth contrasted, in terms of EPI wealth, with those of service industry growth.

During the 1960–73 period, before it too began losing manufacturing jobs, Japan chalked up a prize-winning score of 146 on the EPI. West Germany came next during those years with 124, France scored in the mid-80s, Italy was 67, Sweden 55, the US 50 and Britain registered 43. The same formula for the period of 1974–80, when manufacturing was reeling from OPEC's body blows, gave Japan 38, West Germany 29, the US 15 and Britain a mere 2·2. The difference between the years when manufacturing was strong – the wealth producing years – and those when services took up the jobs slack – the wealth dividing years – is striking. When Britain's score in the first period is placed against that of Japan in the second, it becomes clear that pre-oil shock

Britain had a wealthier, more vital economy than does Japan today.[18]

By 1985, the Manpower Services Commission has warned, a further 1·2 million manufacturing jobs are due to disappear in Britain. It is a figure based on decline rather than collapse and probably makes little allowance for the yet unknown effects of micro-technology. West Germany's more solid and competitive economy, for instance, is threatened with the loss of 4 million jobs to the micro-chip in the 1980s, according to a Prognos study commissioned by the Baden-Württemberg state government. When increasingly cheap technology and expensive labour meet it is not hard to predict the eventual outcome, only the time it will take. What will happen to those displaced workers nobody knows, but it is worth bearing in mind the dictum of Nobel Prize-winning US economist Wassili Leontief: 'The notion that workers being replaced by machines necessarily find employment in the manufacture of these machines is just as absurd as the expectation that horses replaced by automobiles could be needed in the various branches of the automobile industry.'

4

The Micro-electronics Monster

If forecasting unemployment over twelve months, or up to the mid-1980s, is fraught with difficulty, looking toward the 1990s is about as scientific as fortune-telling with tea leaves.

But it is also crucially important to form some assessment of how much work there will be available for people to do ten or fifteen years from now. Governments must shape their policies in the 1980s to dovetail with likely conditions in the following decade, and social attitudes must change to accept that not all people will be able to work.

Predictions of how the revolution in micro-technology will alter matters still differ wildly even though the early seventies micro-chip birth is a decade old. Special reports have ranged from smug assertions that there will be a swings and roundabouts effect so that little will really change, to dramatic warnings of the collapse of a society based on work. And somewhere in the middle of those two extremes there is also the beguiling notion that a new Utopia is at hand, in which 'the machines will do all the work' so that their human masters can devote themselves to lotus-eating.

Before trying to sort the wheat from the chaff of the micro-technology forecasts being made in a number of industrialized countries, it is worthwhile first taking a hard look at that persistent Utopian myth. For whatever it is that the end of the twentieth century has in store it almost certainly does not include a sudden change in human nature or in basic economics. Someone has to pay for, build, instal, service, programme and use high technology machinery. The people who are therefore in work as a result of the new technology become an elite who must decide how much, if any, of their wealth they should distribute to the less fortunate or less skilled who are no longer qualified to work and earn their livings.

In the United States, where buzz-words and jargon are so often coined, the society of the near future is already being split by some academic analysts into two categories – a rich and powerful 'knowledge class' and a 'serf class' which performs menial services. It may sound an unlikely reversal of all the social trends of the last 100 years or more, but it already seems a reality in California where the counterpoint to the 'Silicon Valley' micro-chip boom is an earnest political debate over whether mandatory schooling up to sixteen years-old is really necessary for the children of blacks, hispanics and the poor.

In Europe, the problem is seen in somewhat less stark terms. The issue is how to limit a rapid growth in people who will be the 'have-nots' if their jobs are washed away by the tide of technology.

When trying to estimate the impact of electronics on work it is vital to emphasize that the micro-technology in question is still an unknown quantity. The temptation is to view it as an extension of the mechanical and electrical technology we are used to, when in fact it is more like a bio-genetic monster created by some mad scientist. It changes its nature and its substance before our very eyes and its ever growing tentacles reach out to grasp and transform old industries and traditional work methods. A wordprocessor may be the lineal descendant of a typewriter, but it is a distant cousin with a savage mutant strain.

And the typewriter, it should not be forgotten, was deliberately hamstrung at birth in a way that its solid state successor cannot be. The original keyboard arrangement was seen as too efficient and was re-arranged to slow down the typist. That sort of informal international convention to handicap efficiency is no longer possible, for as the industrial countries grapple for shares of the world market in micro-technology it is breakthroughs in work-saving devices that give them a hold.

Just as important is the point that those countries that do not keep in the forefront of both producing and employing the new technologies eventually lose even more jobs than they at first 'saved' by failing to modernize. In early 1980 the European Commission warned: 'The risk for the Community is that, if we do not innovate as quickly as our industrial competitors, we will lose jobs more rapidly than them, be forced to increase our purchases from them and, by so doing, increase their employment and income at the expense of our own.'[1]

Perhaps one of the earliest victims of this high technology trap was a West German office equipment manufacturing company called Walther Büro-Maschinen that almost ten years ago provided the rest of the European industry with an interesting object lesson. At the start of the 1970s Walther made an all out effort to switch its range of mechanical office calculators to electronic ones, even though that entailed slimming its workforce drastically from 1800 to just 400. It was too little and too late, apparently, for by 1974 the company had collapsed under the pressure of competition from Japan and the US.

According to some experts, though, there is an argument that micro-technology will create almost as many new jobs as it destroys.[2] The view is that, if you were to take two newspapers, one from the early 1950s and the other for today, and compare the situations vacant ads the most striking thing would be the birth of jobs, companies and industries that were not even dreamt of 30 years ago. A rather more reliable guide to developments in the electronics sector is nevertheless more likely to be found in the industry's own recent past. And the evidence so far points to fewer jobs unless the chip and the whole gamut of information technology is leading us towards some still unimagined new industrial dynamic – in other words, a new sort of motor car.

Opinions vary over whether electronics have even provided a boost to employment up until now. The EEC's Brussels Eurocrats assert that over the past decade electronic equipment has been a source of jobs, so that by 1978 the industry employed 2·85 million workers, or 7·5 per cent of the industrial workforce in the Common Market.[3] Yet the employment figures produced by some of the leading corporations in the electronics industry tell a very different story.[4]

Italy's Olivetti commissioned a special study of its international competitors in the 'information products' business, and found that since 1969 the payrolls of the four market leaders in the US, the three in West Germany and itself in Italy had shrunk by an average twenty per cent. Not only that, but Olivetti, which had only shed ten per cent of its workforce, was able to discern that companies that had cut back hardest, such as West Germany's Olympia Werke with a 35 per cent loss of jobs, were also making a good deal of the running with new and non-mechanical electronic goods.

It may be that the switch-over from electrically operated mechanical devices to solid state 'no moving parts' electronics is clouding the issue, for it has resulted so far in lay-offs of metal workers and mechanics and the creation instead of much more compact production units that are centred around systems analysts and computer programmers rather than precision engineers. But if factories producing the new electronics goods eventually provide work for almost as many people as the old style machine shops – which is what the most optimistic forecasters suggest – it is even more certain that the high technology companies still have a good deal more workers to shed. Telecommunications, the jewel in the crown of the hi-tech revolution, is a case in point.

Leaving aside, for the moment, the snowballing sci-fi visions of computer networks that send mail by coaxial cables, let us turn to the common or garden telephone. There are basically three types of telephone exchange switching systems and by the end of the 1980s almost all advanced countries plan to have abandoned the two that are predominantly in use in favour of the third and electronic one that is available. The job implications of this modernization are, to say the least, profound.

A little background: Type I, the oldest of the automatic systems for switching telephone calls, is the electromechanical rotary device such as the Strowger system used in the UK. In micro-chip terms it is an antique and according to the latest figures it still accounts for an average of almost 90 per cent of all switching equipment in West Germany, the UK, Switzerland, Holland, Belgium and Italy. Japan still uses it to the tune of about nineteen per cent and the US just over a quarter.[5]

The odd-man-out in Europe is France, which relies on the Type I 'step by step' system for only 27 per cent or so of its 'phone calls. And that is because France was for long so notoriously behind on telecommunications – General de Gaulle had dismissed the 'phone as 'un gadget' – that the French together with the Japanese were able to lead the world with the introduction of Type II, the much more advanced 'Crossbar' switching system. But the micro-chip, thanks to its flexibility and its ever increasing cheapness, has now produced Type III in the shape of fully electronic digital transmission equipment that is so versatile and cost-effective that it makes the scrapping of Types I & II an economic must.

For System X, as the new generation of electronic exchange equipment is called in Britain, is to be an invaluable telecommunications infrastructure. It will provide the ganglia of nerves needed to link up the electronic brains of the future.

The advent of Type III would at first sight seem to promise a welcome boost to employment in the telecommunications industry in Europe, while also helping it to regain some of the ground lost to American and Japanese competition. Unfortunately, the use of electronic equipment to produce electronic equipment has already cut swathes through the ranks of the equipment producers' workforces and threatens greater mayhem to come.

One estimate quoted in a study by the UK's Department of

Employment suggests that while 26 people were employed to produce a Type I or II unit of a certain capacity, the production of a semi-electronic unit handling the same level of traffic needed only ten workers and a fully electronic System X unit could be built by only one.[6] The American example is the most illuminating – not least because during the 1970s the US made giant strides and installed enough Type III equipment to handle over 30 per cent of all telephone calls, while the average in other countries is still less than two per cent. There the Bell System's manufacturing arm, the world-leading AT&T now re-named Western Electric, chopped its workforce by more than half between 1970 and 1980.[7]

Just as grim for the jobs outlook is the telex, which cannot be separated from the telecommunications revolution. Since it went electronic there have been trades union warnings that up to 80 per cent of jobs in telex production may eventually be axed. So far, Siemens has found that although its output of electronic telexes has of late trebled, it has also had to cut employment on that side by twenty per cent.[8]

And what of the operators of the telephone systems? Britain's Post Office, which cut back by a third in the five years up to 1978 on the number of telephonists it employs, nevertheless hopes to maintain constant levels of employment.[9] France's new government is even looking to the PTT as a 'market sensitive' part of the public sector where increased demand might possibly swell employment.[10] In Holland, a report prepared for the Dutch government has suggested that the telecommunications boom will at least mean more maintenance jobs,[11] even though Western Electric's own assessment is that System III exchanges entail the loss of 75 per cent of jobs in maintenance, repairs and installation.[12]

If the makers and the operators of comparatively straightforward equipment such as new-style telephone systems find it hard to sort out what it all means, the chaos of conflicting views amongst the potential users of the new micro-technology is predictably awesome. Will the micro-tech revolution hit offices harder than factories? Or the unskilled harder than those with traditional mechanical skills? Youth rather than experience? Or will it, in all these cases, be the other way around?

As nobody really knows, let us start first with fundamentals before examining the various assertions that are being made. The name of the game in any economy, any business activity, is costs. If costs can be kept right down, an operation can undercut the competition and enter the virtuous circle of profitability and expansion. Costs divide broadly into capital equipment and labour, and it is with the relative expense of those two items that the high technology phenomenon spells trouble.

Until very recently, capital equipment cost a good deal more than labour. Some experts reckon that until the micro-processor became established, the mechanical equipment needed to displace labour cost an average of at least ten times the annual cost of that labour, and in some cases could rise to 100 times as much. An employer had to think very carefully before automating.[13]

Now such calculations have almost overnight been scrapped, and the tumbling price of technology still has a long way to fall. Micro-computer items that were produced for about a dollar each in 1980 are expected to cost only 10–20 cents by 1985.[14] And even in 1980 terms the technology is already considerably cheaper than labour. An industrial robot designed to do skilled fitting work in a car assembly plant currently costs about $40,000, and when its round-the-clock life over eight years is broken down into servicing costs and depreciation charges, its hourly 'wage bill' works out at less than five dollars as against the fifteen dollars earned by a Detroit worker.[15] In Sweden's Saab-Scania car plant, a robot that does the work of two men is now reckoned to pay for itself in fifteen months, and one that replaces three workers pays for itself in eighteen months.[16] The arithmetic would be simple to apply to a host of industries, were it not that the robots are getting cheaper as labour becomes more expensive.

With labour being priced out of the market at such an accelerating rate, the priority must be to assess which types of work are most at risk. It is a task made no easier by the fact that almost all the analyses of different sectors represent some sort of special pleading – some trades unions try Canute-like to turn the tide with 'scare' reports, while some government-initiated ones attempt to pretend that there really is no problem as it is not readily quantifiable.

First, the broad brush strokes. Blue-collar or white-collar? Most probably office jobs will evaporate the fastest during the 1980s, with factory jobs bearing the brunt of a second and even more determined attack wave by the robots in the 1990s.

According to a study undertaken by Siemens, though never formally published, almost half of all clerical jobs in West Germany will be affected by micro-electronic information handling at some point during the 1980s. And that presumably goes for the 15 million wholly clerical jobs that are reckoned to exist throughout the EEC. The Siemens 'Office 1990' report reckoned that the new equipment would mean average productivity gains in office work of 2·2–3·5 per cent a year, and inside that framework over 40 per cent of tasks would become highly standardized, with inevitable job losses, while 25–30 per cent of tasks would be automated out of existence.[17]

Siemens' productivity figures, however, are on the low side for some types of office work. The replacement of the typewriter by word-processors implies a considerably higher rate of job loss. IBM, the US electronics colossus, has estimated that word-processors can increase a typist's productivity by 150 per cent,[18] and the British clerical union APEX has warned that a shared facility word-processing machine with several terminals can boost productivity by 300 per cent.[19] Drawing numbers out of the air, a French analysis has forecast a 20–25 reduction in the number of secretaries that will be needed, and the Geneva-based FIET clerical trades union umbrella organization[20] has forecast that a productivity growth rate of eight per cent a year in office work would make 5 million of Western Europe's 17–18 million clerical workers redundant by the end of the decade.[21] Taking numbers, rather less dramatically, from experience, a local authority office in Yorkshire cut its typing staff from 39 to 19 with a word-processing system, and Norway's Storebrand has over 25 years used technology to cut clerical jobs by five-sixths.[22]

Many of those jobs went quite recently, with the arrival of word-processors. But Storebrand's track record is at odds with most companies in the financial services sector, who have been increasingly large employers since World War II, and raises the question of what micro-electronics will do to banking and all the other labour intensive financial activities. Banks in Common Market countries, for instance, boosted their payrolls by around 70 per cent during the last twenty years and now employ almost 5 million people.[23]

At a glance, most banking and money transmission looks overripe for the electronic sickle. In fact it is rather more complicated than that, not least because banks tend to occupy privileged positions inside national economies, and can be sheltered from foreign competition, and also because bank employees' trade unions are increasingly muscular. Much the same goes for their counterparts in the civil services, where (irony of ironies) militants have shown that it is easy to nobble the computers to press home a demand. In Britain in 1979 Post Office employees 'locked' £1 billion worth of 'phone bills inside the computer that eventually took six costly months to clear; the following year a NALGO strike halted all local government rate demands within 48 hours and within the first week of the 1981 Civil Service disruptions four-fifths of the government's weekly VAT take of £250 million went uncollected.[24] Providing – and it is a major proviso – that the 'knowledge class' employees, who have access to the big administrative combines' computers, remain loyal to their less qualified clerical colleagues, new technology could be slowed down.

The picture in financial services is further confused by the fact that banking and insurance are still growing, although not as fast as productivity theoretically could. The Simon Nora-Alain Minc report to the French government foresaw a 30 per cent job loss in insurance over the next ten years and a similar saving through 'wastage' in banking.[25]

But all these dire predictions are based merely on equipment that is by and large generally available. The implications of systems that are shortly to be introduced are even more serious. For example, Xerox Corporation's Palo Alto research centre in northern California has designed, installed and operated a system that appears to reduce office workers to a skeleton staff of white coated technicians who would handle the equipment that serves the decision-making executives. Called 'Ethernet', it also by-passes the postal system by transmitting mail by coaxial cable while on a more humdrum level it links up personal desktop minicomputers with typewriters, printers, file storages, copiers, text-processors and major central computers.[26]

If the spectre of an office almost devoid of people and filled instead with gently humming machinery is not enough, some forecasters dispute the idea that blue-collar work will be less immediately affected than clerical and administrative jobs. One expert, Sir Ieuan Maddock, has predicted that in the UK the manufacturing sector looks the most vulnerable to the microprocessor. He sees the 7·25 million workers employed in Britain's manufacturing industries being reduced to less than 5 million, 'and perhaps much less', by the turn of the century and is very doubtful that any new manufacturing industries could absorb those laid-off.[27]

Some American long range forecasts are more striking still. Peter Drucker has claimed that it is 'practically certain – barring nuclear war' that the US manufacturing sector will in 25 years time be little larger than the agricultural sector. That means that the 20 million Americans now in manufacturing would be shrunk to somewhere between 7 million and 12 million.[28]

If the same forecast were applied to the EEC labour market, which is roughly the same size, it is certain that electronics production would not make up the gap. The Brussels Commission sees computer industry workers in the EEC only doubling to 400,000 by 1985.[29]

Behind all these definitions of which broad categories of jobs are the most vulnerable, there is the equally important question of what sort of people are most at risk. And some of the findings produced by researchers are surprising. Because less privileged members of our 'work society' – blacks, women, disabled, unskilled and so on – are notoriously the first to be pushed out of work by most pressures, the general assumption has been that they would be the first victims of the micro-chip.

The trend, in fact, tends to be the reverse. Or to be more accurate, the trend tends to be that the unskilled and the super-skilled can live with electronics, while the people who are either skilled in traditional engineering or who have skills that electronic equipment does more accurately and cheaply are the first to be displaced. If you wanted to place a somewhat political tag on it, you might well say that the 'cream of the working class', after at the very least a century of being the aristocrats of the shopfloor, will be first into the tumbrils of the hi-tech revolution. And their removal into the limbo of what is now being called the 'post-industrial society' means that there may well be a California-style polarisation yielding a 'knowledge class' and the serfs. A good example of how the unskilled and semi-skilled workers edged out the previously dominant skilled workforce was provided not long ago by an ITT company called Standard Electric Lorenz. In switching over to electronic telex machine production it replaced 936 parts in the electromechanical version with a single micro-processor, and at the same time transformed its own shopfloor. Jobs requiring training dropped from 82 per cent to just 35 per cent, semi-skilled ones that had only been 15 per cent rose to 35 per cent and at the highly skilled end, men in white coats, it jumped from two per cent to 30 per cent.[30]

That leap in the combined strength of unskilled labour and highly qualified technicians as a proportion of the workforce is significant. At the ITT plant it jumped from only 17 per cent of the payroll to 65 per cent, and reduced the skilled craftsmen who usually make up the bulk of a factory's workforce to a minority.

The vulnerability of skilled workers to 'smart' technology is becoming plain enough. But there are many other jobs now unexpectedly joining factory and office ones on the list of high risk occupations. Like the industrial and clerical worker, they also represent considerable political muscle. For small businesses, together with the smaller, local outlets of larger businesses, are also potential victims of high technology. Retailing, which in Western Europe, the US and particularly Japan, has in the past provided a valuable source of employment, looks set for drastic slimming.

During the 1970s, retailing is reckoned in Europe to have shed about five per cent of its jobs, largely as a result of supermarket pressure.[31] And in the 1980s it is feared that the larger retail chains' ability to take advantage of cost-cutting electronic systems will not only cut their workforces but will squeeze the High Street small fry even harder. The same not only goes for smaller manufacturing and even craft businesses, it also applies to the big banks' smaller branches, where electronic automation does not at present seem worth the investment cost and closures look inevitable.

How far one should take all these dire predictions it is very hard to say. At the start of this chapter I described the state of the art as fortune-telling with tea leaves, so perhaps one should at least record what a few of the more prominent and daring sooth-sayers have predicted. First, though, a word of warning. The following figures are what economists call 'mechanical estim-ations', meaning that they are often grossly over-simplified arithmetical exercises that take little or no account of the plastic and flexible qualities of an economy. Possibly the best example of how dramatic, and yet unimaginative, such calculations can be is a French estimate that new office technology could lead to a 6 million rise in unemployment in that country. It was arrived at by assuming a 100 per cent productivity rise that halved 12 million office jobs there.[32]

Other estimates range from the Rand Corporation's extrapol-ation of industrial trends up to the end of the century to forecast a US manufacturing base shrunk to just two per cent of the work-force, to a West German estimate that UK unemployment will hit fifteen per cent by 1985 and twenty per cent in 1990.[33] Possibly the most workmanlike attempt to analyse the UK jobs future – even though its semi-mechanical nature has led to charges that it was 'adding apples and oranges' – was made by the Association of Scientific, Technical and Managerial Staffs. Clive Jenkins, the ASTMS General Secretary, and Barrie Sherman, its Research Director, selected 27 employment categories for the economy and calculated job losses in each. The sample labour force of 22·36 million in 1978 had by end-1983 dropped just over 1 million to 21·34 million and in 1993 was down to 18·56 million. In the year 2003 it stood at 17·14 million, or a drop over 25 years of 23 per cent. The study also stated what it saw as the basic dilemma: 'Remain as we are, reject the new technologies and we face unemployment of up to 5·5 million by the end of the century. Embrace the new technologies, accept the challenge, and we end up with unemployment of about 5 million.'[34]

On rather safer ground, there have also been attempts to assess the proportion of jobs lying in the path of the micro-electronic juggernaut. One of the highest estimates is in the same ASTMS study, and puts 62 per cent of all occupations at some risk. A report for the West German government by the Swiss consultants Prognos put the figure at up to half of all job-types, a figure that a number of authorities do not quarrel with, including the 'think tank' analysts on the UK's Central Policy Review Staff. At the Paris-based Organization for Economic Co-operation and Development (OECD), however, officials take a more cautious line and put their estimate at 32 per cent.[35]

So there it is. In round figures the experts put the impact of the micro-chip at anywhere between one-third and two-thirds of all jobs. In terms of the Common Market workforce, or that of the US which is roughly the same size, that means a low of around 35 million people are at risk, rising to a high of almost 70 million. And that is based on the view from the early 1980s foothills of the technological mountain, for the peaks of the 1990s remain hidden from sight.

Of Scroungers and Suicides

In a seedy cafe close by the cathedral in Metz, Simon Robert was explaining what it is like to be down and out in Lorraine. Nursing a cup of cold coffee, the 39-year old out-of-work printing operative went through the francs and centimes of unemployment benefit in France. As he spoke it became clear that it is not the cash levels that bothered him so much – by British standards the benefits are comparatively generous in spite of some recent cutbacks – but the grudging, institutionalized charity that losing his job forces him to ask for.

Simon Robert is a nervous, almost surly, man. To look at he seems closer to 50 than 40. It is less than a year since he lost his job of eight years running an offset machine at the state-run 'Maison des Jeunes' in Metz, and there is already an aura of failure about him. Judging by his comments, it was not so much the sacking itself that he found demoralizing but his inability to find other work since then. Dismissal caused by austerity measures had an impersonal quality; continued failure to secure a new job does not.

Nowadays, he has care and custody of his two children, aged 11 and 13. Under the French system he can go on netting about three-quarters of his former salary until they have left school. It means a fairly tight budget, but he can cope. His job used to pay 3600 francs a month net (about £450), and family allowances total a further 520 francs a month. Since signing on for unemployment benefit in October 1980 he has been receiving 2500 francs a month, so that with family allowances total income has gone from 4120 francs a month to 3020 francs. When his year of 'indemnisation', or dole insurance, is up he can apply to a social security tribunal for rent and child allowances totalling 1800 francs that together with his much more meagre 750 francs a month dole money could bring his income back to around 3000 francs. As he pays 1200 francs in rent, he couldn't live on less.

The most striking thing about Simon Robert, though, is not his money worries or even his resentment at the way in which, after a year on the dole, he becomes a charity case rather than someone with a right to draw insurance. It is his helplessness. Talking about himself and his future he seemed deeply uncertain about whether he is a printer who, with a little luck, will once again find a job in the printing industry, or whether he was once a printer in the same way that during his twenties he had once been a lorry driver. As jobs in transport are if anything even scarcer than jobs in printing, because there are so many unskilled men looking for work, reverting to his former occupation is not the answer. 'Je suis chômeur', he concluded, thus acknowledging that his occupation now is simply to be unemployed.

It was not a very satisfactory answer, either to himself, in its admission that he no longer has any useful role to perform, or to the French taxpayers who are supporting him at 75 per cent of his former income. Less than 40 years old, with a family to support and a trade that should enable him to do that, Simon Robert is getting a raw deal. And so too, maybe, is the taxpayer, for there is no way of knowing whether Robert could or would take a general labouring job if the safety net of benefits did not exist.

So who and what are the unemployed? Rich man, poor man, beggarman, thief; scrounger, victim, weakling, cheat? How are they going to fit into society in the future, and, as work gets harder to come by, what sort of deal will those with jobs grant those without? Attitudes to the unemployed are fuzzy and sometimes deeply contradictory, running a confusing gamut from sentimental mawkishness to resentment and indifference. The confusion is natural enough in a social system so firmly based on work, and in which the pecking order is fixed by occupation.

When there was no structural shortage of work, that lack of a coherent social, and therefore political, approach to joblessness was unimportant. During most of the post-war years the real unemployed were generally the unemployable. But now it is beginning to matter a lot. Trained graduates, impressionable teenagers, liberated women, skilled craftsmen and experienced executives are all joining the ranks of the inadequate, the work-shy, the moonlighters and the totally unskilled to make a non-sense of the blanket term 'unemployed'.

Society's natural prejudice is that each fit member should be able to earn a living. 'Them as don't work, don't eat' was the motto, and it seemed fair enough at that. But if there are not enough livings to go around, so that employment becomes a lottery in which 35 million people in the OECD countries are the losers, who is to say what is still fair? Stabs at fair-mindedness only tend to muddle matters more. Perhaps the two best examples are 'Attitude I', that unemployment in this day and age is in no sense comparable with unemployment in the 1930s, and 'Attitude II', that anyway a lot of present day unemployment is made up of women who do not really need to work.

That first attitude, the widely held view in Britain that the 1981 total of 3 million registered unemployed is not comparable with the peak of almost 3 million at the start of the 'Hungry Thirties', is correct in one sense. As the workforce was that much smaller it represented joblessness of 22 per cent among male heads of households, so that together with tighter dole qualifications almost a quarter of the country's population was reduced to abject poverty. But the income gap between people in work and those on the dole was at the same time much narrower then than it is now. Unemployment benefit in Britain is currently at its lowest level in relation to average earnings for some time, and compared to the 1930s the gap has widened to a chasm.[1]

Recent research at the London School of Economics has shown that while in real terms the average industrial wage now buys twice as much as it did 50 years ago, unemployment benefit in the UK for a family with three children buys only 25 per cent more than the list of rock bottom subsistence goods drawn up by Rowntree in 1936.[2] No feather bedding there.

Attitude II, that a substantial proportion of the unemployed consists of women who are not heads of a household, is thought to be one of the chief reasons in Europe and America that concern over unemployment has not given way to real anxiety. Yet soaring divorce rates and the consequent rise in the numbers of single parent families should long ago have cut the ground away from beneath the 'male breadwinner' prejudice. In the US almost half the 42 million women who are such an important part of the 106 million total labour force are now supporting either a family or themselves.[3] In Europe the trend is towards a similar proportion of female breadwinners by the mid-1980s.

The fact that unemployment benefits are not being paid out on a lavish scale, and cannot be seen as a useful supplement to the breadwinner's wages, is not saving the dole from political pressures to reduce the scale of payments. In the UK, West Germany and the US there is a mood of unsympathetic determination that government spending deficits could reasonably be lightened by cutting benefit levels. It is an oddly contradictory trend, for the argument seems to be that when joblessness was less of a problem governments could afford to pay fairly handsome benefit levels, but now that so many people are becoming unemployed the expense will be prohibitive.

Yet the amount paid in dole, and the conditions attached, are going to be crucially important in the next few years. They sum up society's attitude to unemployment, and therefore to those people who will be ill-favoured or merely unfortunate enough not to be paying their way. As things stand, the dole system will be grotesquely unsuited to the needs of many of the more adequate people who will be without work.

Unemployment benefits of one sort or another are not the right financial instruments for funding joblessness of the scale and type that the 1980s are bringing. The dole and its associated welfare payments are no more than a temporary insurance that has served to tide over the unemployed during the fairly short time that, since the late 1940s, has elapsed for most people between losing one job and finding another. The suspicion that not a few people took advantage of that insurance to avail themselves of a between-jobs holiday at the state's expense has contributed towards the resentment with which the dole and the unemployed are now regarded.

In Britain, before the recession and the jobs crisis began to frighten people into staying put, as many as 10 million people, or almost two-fifths of the labour force, often changed jobs during a single year. The figures are probably distorted a bit by 'temp' typists and reflect, too, a healthy upward mobility in which people were trading-up in their work. But they are also thought to have meant that all too many were deliberately dropping into the dole queues for a while. Abuses by what is probably no more than a fairly small fraction of those who have ever claimed unemployment benefit have in many minds clouded the issue. Stricter policing of the dole does not make the benefits system more equitable.

Cutting back the number of people in the limbo of the dole queues is clearly part of the answer to squabbles over benefit levels, and that will lend a good deal of weight to demands for work-sharing and 'make work' schemes that are examined in Chapter 8. As occupation equals identity for most people, and as society is anyway footing the bill for the unemployed, the idea of finding occupations that do not necessarily command labour market wages seems an attractive one. But it has drawbacks that are as much social as they are economic.

The principal one is that even if unemployment were to exceed the direst predictions and go to twenty per cent, there would still be a labour market consisting of four people of working age out of five. How do you have a large minority of one-fifth carrying on their uneconomic activities while the four-fifths who are paying for it all are still stuck in the rat race? How do those in 'real' work fix their wage rates if the people in 'make believe' work are being paid anything like the same? Like any good conundrum, it all gets more baffling the more you walk around it. If, in an attempt to be fair to those unlucky enough to lose the employment lottery of the 1980s, the wages for this parallel work are fixed anywhere close to market pay rates, to what extent will people 'transfer' between the real economy and the voluntary parallel economy? In theory they could move in and out – a grocer could opt to do a spell at a macro-biotic health foods co-operative, a joiner could go into artisanal arts and crafts, a highly skilled engineering operative might choose to run training courses for deprived and alienated teenagers in a black ghetto. The list of useful and enriching possibilities is endless and they all run up against the same snag. Everyone knows that the real economy is the one that counts, so almost all the people who switch to the voluntary one risk acknowledging their own lack of worth. Apart from rare acts of quixoticism, most people invited to leave their jobs for the make-believe economy would feel that they had become unimportant. Underlying it all, there is the fact of economic life that in the foreseeable future even highly advanced post-industrial societies cannot afford a system that does not discriminate between earners and others.

The whole argument therefore tends to come down to one between the economists and the sociologists, which is the same thing as a difference of opinion between powerful treasury experts in a finance ministry and supplicants in a 'spending' ministry. The sociologists are nevertheless a valuable guide to the pressures now building up, for the minimalist view is of an unhappy and more deeply divided society.

In cold cash, many of the employed are already doing no better than the unemployed. Researchers for Britain's Low Pay Unit pointed out in mid-1981 that unskilled manual workers are now earning less in relation to average earnings in the UK than in 1886, when figures were first collated. In fact, 30 per cent of the country's full-time adult workforce is now in the low-paid bracket, which gives a total of 4·75 million people, while in the part-time sector 2·75 million people, or over 60 per cent of part-timers, are also in the very poorly paid category. Taken together with the registered unemployed in Britain of around 3 million, the picture that emerges is one of two-fifths of the labour force at or under a £75-a-week breadline.

And none of this takes account of the 'discouraged', those potential workers, often women who withdraw from the statistically observable labour force. That usually means that they have, for one reason or another, no right to unemployment benefit, and so disappear from the ken of the civil servants. In the UK the discouraged are put at about 1 million people by trade union leaders such as TUC general secretary Len Murray, and in other European countries as well as the US they are generally believed to add a further twenty per cent or so to the registered unemployed. In Brussels it is reckoned that at least 1 million of the 8 million young people due to come on to the jobs market by 1985 will be discouraged and so will never show up in the figures.

But there is also a growing appreciation that in a jobs crisis of the dimension now apparent, discouraged workers can be a blessing in disguise. Political point-makers may use them for headlines like 'Maggie's Missing Million' or as an indictment of unemployment figures being fudged, but the discouraged are often people who can move easily from employment to household work without suffering intense personal problems. Working wives who are forced back into being housewives may have financial problems but at least they also have a role to revert to.

For those who have no substitute role, being put out of work can have devastating side effects. Research into the human toll of rising unemployment has of late been building up a stark and disturbing picture of suffering that runs from suicide to heart disease, divorce to mental illness and social alienation to criminal behaviour. In Britain, a massive survey of the unemployed found not long ago that for most of the 8000 people polled, the shock of losing their jobs constituted 'the worst thing that ever happened' to them in their lives.[4]

As the unemployed go downhill, many of them also take it out on their families. In the US, the University of Michigan at Ann Arbor is now mounting a research drive into such fringe effects as drug abuse, domestic violence and alcoholism. Other American

academics are even trying to quantify the human costs of joblessness. In Maryland, at Johns Hopkins University, Baltimore,
Professor M. Harvey Brenner has been studying the health consequences of unemployment since the early 1970s, and has lately
produced figures, based on demographic data, suggesting that
37,000 deaths result directly from each one per cent increase in
the US unemployment rate.[5]

As the European Community's workforce is about the same
size as that of the US, Brenner's figures could mean that since
1974 joblessness may have cost up to 200,000 lives in the EEC
countries, and that a further quarter of a million lives will be
forfeit during the 1980s. Brenner's ability to come up with precise figures for such a nebulous condition as unemployment,
when so many variables abound, tends to strain one's faith
somewhat. But he calculates that over a six year period each
percentage point rise in the jobless rate has the following effect:
20,240 deaths from cardiovascular disease, 920 suicides, 648
homicides and 495 deaths from cirrhosis of the liver. Various
other categories raise the toll to precisely 36,887. Some US
experts are vaguer but more emphatic. 'I'm now convinced that
unemployment is *the* killer disease in this country', says Thomas
Cottle of the Harvard Medical School, 'responsible for wife
beating, infertility and even tooth decay.'[6]

Research in Britain is arriving at similar conclusions. In Scotland, which tops the world league for deaths from heart disease,
a special health education group has been studying the relationship between high unemployment and coronary deaths. Its
head, Dr David Player, believes the link is 'significant'. A former President of the British Medical Association, Professor
Lindford Rees, has described the shock of unemployment as
similar to that of suffering a close family bereavement. He cited
reports that the jobless suffer 'much higher levels of anxiety,
guilt, hostility, self-criticism and personal distress'.[7]

Rather like a jigsaw puzzle once it starts to take shape, much of
this research in different countries is beginning to provide con-
firmation of a trend or to fill in important gaps. The survey of

8000 jobless over a year, carried out in the UK by the Policy Studies Institute and mentioned earlier, found that, even in the early stages, unemployment has a measurable impact on health. Depression and an inability to eat or sleep in the first six weeks on the dole were symptoms reported by fourteen per cent of the sample, while the stress effects that build up, and are much more important, were very widely cited in the later stages. A leading American psychologist provides a cross-reference with the finding that 'nine months seems to be a crucial point', after the loss of work, 'when hope and patience give out'.[8] Stress is seen to be the key underlying factor, as much responsible for the 30 per cent increase in child battering for which the NSPCC in Britain singled out unemployment as a cause,[9] as for the findings by US experts that unemployment blackspots produce a suicide rate that is 30 times the American national average.[10]

Some British research, though, is delving even more deeply into the social effects of dwindling employment than this often predictable catalogue of mental and physical illness. It is still too early to tell, but they may be finding some surprising changes in young people's attitudes to work and wealth and hearth and home.

Ray Pahl, Professor of Sociology at the University of Kent, has been studying the effects of mounting unemployment on the Isle of Sheppey, chosen because it is a fairly isolated and self-contained community with one of the highest jobless rates in south east England. Less than ten per cent of school-leavers get apprenticeships or places in higher education, up to 30 per cent can be on the dole and the rest are unskilled labour. He suspects that a strange topsy-turvy shift may be taking place, in which the young women are becoming more work-oriented and the young men may be turning away from work toward the family 'as a main source of identity'. Pahl stresses that it is all very impressionistic and that his conclusions are only tentative, but he suggests that 'the boys fear unemployment and lack of respect. The girls fear the trap of being a household mother'. In an article reporting his early findings, he observed: 'I think that in areas such as the one I am working in, women will play an increasingly dominant role in employment. Talking to the adults, the women seem much more ready to commit themselves to a life of paid employment. The men tell me that they soon intend to pack it in. They don't enjoy their work; they are bored and frustrated. If it is poorly paid, they calculate the disadvantages in terms of early starts, long hours, the cost of the journey to work, the noise and the dirt in the factory, the amount of tax they pay, the way they are treated by their boss. "I'd be better off on the dole" seems objectively accurate if everything is taken into account. For those who are more highly paid there again seems to be little commitment. The work is described as boring and undignified.'

These social attitudes are such unfamiliar territory that it is hard to know if what Pahl thinks he is seeing is worth believing. For a start there is, for the young and single, some sort of magnet in the dole. There are also a number of other factors that must be reckoned with.

Paul Osterman, Assistant Professor of Economics at Boston University, has come up with a 'moratorium' theory that may help to explain why teenagers both reject work and figure so disproportionately in the dole queues. His research in the Boston, Massachusetts area led him to conclude: 'When young people leave high school and enter the labour market, they are generally not at once in a state of mind to be stable, reliable full time employees. Rather, for many youths, sex, adventure and peer group activities are more important than work. Jobs are viewed in purely instrumental terms, as ways of getting money for these other activities. Young people who exhibit this pattern of behaviour can be characterized as being in a "moratorium" stage. They have weak labour force attachments, frequently moving in and out of jobs as well as of the labour force itself.'[11] Other American academics who have been studying the question point out that amongst underprivileged black teenagers, where unemployment is in the 40 per cent-plus range, the belief that through minor fiddles they can 'beat the system' helps make joblessness more attractive.[12]

Researchers elsewhere have been concentrating on whether increasing long term joblessness is creating a new 'sub-society' of people who are being pushed into withdrawing from the mainstream of life. Work at Belgium's University of Louvain has produced an illuminating study that provides ammunition both for liberals seeking to alleviate the plight of the unemployed and for conservatives determined to tackle the scroungers issue.

According to Magda Lambert, the project director, the Louvain survey identified four very different categories of unemployed. The first of these is the 'pseudo-unemployed', who accounted for about a quarter of the survey's sample and whose lives were scarcely affected at all by joblessness. Indeed, most saw dole money as a form of semi-legitimate income. They ranged from those who saw benefits as a bonus on top of undeclared earnings in the 'black economy' to others who could morally justify taking the money but used it for other purposes than was intended.

The examples include university students who register as unemployed and then use their dole money as a 'scholarship' while carrying out post-graduate work, men who have retired prematurely who see social security as a form of pension, and women who have stopped work and reverted to the role of housewife and mother, who regard unemployment benefit as a supplement to the family allowance. Belgium's own rather liberal system for granting dole payments – it puts no time limit, even on women who are not the heads of a household – may tend to encourage abuses, but the moral justifications for scrounging are nevertheless interesting.

The Louvain study began with the intention of fleshing out what was felt to be the rather sweeping but commonly held view that there were basically two types of unemployed, the scroungers and the real victims. It discovered that there were in fact three types of victims and that over time the unemployed could shift from one category to another. The survey selected at random 100 case studies, and, to observe these changes, re-interviewed people after six months.

The study's second category, the first of the three 'victim' types, was those unemployed who are looking for work. Magda Lambert described people in this as the 'most pure' type of unemployed, for whom re-establishing a work role is personally vital. The unemployed in this Category II often refuse to admit to their own families that they have lost their jobs until it becomes impossible to hide, and as a result are often the most likely to find another job quickly. But if, even after only a month on the dole, work cannot be found, a person in this 'temporarily unemployed' category quickly begins to go downhill and is liable to transfer to Category III – those who have become reconciled to not working.

This third section of the unemployed is for many people also a transitory one, for it consists of those who can live with their unemployment without too much unhappiness. To do so, however, they must often take a conscious decision that work and life are not the same things, which for many amounts to assuming a new identity, and usually this involved developing an important spare time activity that helped provide them with that fresh role in life.

Failure to re-adjust in that way means that the unemployed person passes through Category III to the fourth and final category, which is that of the 'traumatized unemployed'. It is also possible to by-pass Category III completely and move straight from II into IV. Yet it is important to prevent the jobless person from becoming traumatized because by then, leaving aside any physical or mental problems that may develop, he has become alienated from work. For both categories III and IV still feel themselves to be looking for work, if not as intensively as Category II, and, while type III can easily return to work if it is available, type IV often finds it hard if not impossible. He may begin another job, but is liable to lose it within a short space of time. This is partly a reflection of the tensions that have built up during his time on the dole – there is, for example, the major problem of 'territory', in which both wife and children resent having the man of the house around during the day, and that further emphasises his lack of a role – but it also results from the fact that a new job is often inferior to the original one.

American analysts at the University of Michigan contend that the tensions created by taking a replacement job at lower pay and with lower status make matters worse. They can create what is called a 'bumping and skidding' pattern of downward mobility that is very damaging to mental health. Economists, incidentally, call that sort of displacement 'churning' and agree it is no solution to the jobs crisis.

The lesson that the Louvain study team are drawing from their research is that it is crucial to distinguish between Categories III and IV when considering therapy treatment for depression stemming from unemployment. So far, mental health therapy for the jobless has not developed on a concerted scale, although a few unemployment blackspots in Michigan such as the stricken community of Fond du Lac have set up their own therapy centres in what could become pilots for other towns. The Belgian project's finding was, though, that group therapy sessions are only adequate for Category III unemployed, and that intense and individual therapy methods are needed to achieve positive results with the seriously traumatized jobless of Category IV.

Although the loss of a working role and of the time frame that a working day provides both seem very much at the roots of the psychological problems of the unemployed, most people on the dole see a single factor as the cause of their stress; money. The major British survey of unemployed people mentioned earlier, carried out by the Policy Studies Institute over a year beginning in May 1980, found that, for 78 per cent of those still out of work after six weeks, financial difficulties had become their 'overwhelming worry'. Contrary to the fairly widespread belief that a good many of the workers who become unemployed at least have a lump sum of redundancy money to cushion them, the Policy Studies Institute put the proportion of unemployed with any sort of a golden handshake at seventeen per cent, while a UK Department of Employment survey in 1980 said the figure could work out at less than ten per cent.[13]

The issue of benefits as a whole is nevertheless becoming the focus for increasingly heated debate in industrialized countries over the status and just deserts of the unemployed. It is the point at which those who press the 'victims' case, and those who cry 'scroungers', clash head on. And yet, for all that, it is a grey and murky area where there are few clear cut rights and wrongs.

Scroungers must have been around as long as time, with Dickens' Artful Dodger the scion of an undistinguished line. But the welfare state saw the birth of a new breed of suspected scrounger, with unexpectedly hilarious results. In 1947 the Attlee government decided that there were up to 1·5 million spivs and scroungers idling around who could be usefully employed in industry and the coal mines. It asked Scotland Yard 'to help round up the work dodgers', and at one point the Cabinet apparently pondered the bizarre idea of banning the football pools in order to release their clerical employees for work in the textile industry. In the end, after a political furore over a 'dictator law' aimed at press-ganging the 'drones', it was discovered that a statistical discrepancy was largely responsible for Attlee's 'missing million' workers.[14]

It is an instructive tale, for if nothing else it points up the difference between myth and reality when dealing with the scroungers issue. But every now and again a prime example hits the headlines to prove that scrounging is rather more than a resilient myth. The essence of scrounging is, of course, that life on the dole can be more attractive and better rewarded than work, and that the system is so lax that the unscrupulous can easily exploit it. Misleading though they may be, there have lately been two cases that confirm those two prejudices. In the US there have notoriously been about 450,000 laid-off workers who, thanks to a twenty-year old scheme for cushioning industry against import penetration and job losses, have been earning more than when they were employed.[15]

In Britain not long ago, passions were aroused in the House of Commons when the Press published details of a real Italian caper. It concerned a pamphlet put out by a Left-wing co-operative in Venice that explained how under EEC arrangements European visitors to Britain could enjoy a 'six-month free holiday'. Apart from run-of-the-mill unemployment benefit and a rent allowance, the booklet estimated that further discretionary payments for clothing, heating, furniture and 'indispensable accessories' could boost the scrounging tourists' take to £250 a month.[16]

It is quite obvious that neither of these examples is a true reflection of life on the dole. But they help create a climate of opinion in which government cuts in benefit levels become politically acceptable, and in which dark suspicions of the mobilization of a 'benefits police' breed fears of a 1930s-style institutionalized means test. As it is, the abolition of earnings-related supplementary benefit covering the unemployed for the first six months pushes Britain firmly to the bottom of the European league table for unemployment benefits in relation to previous earnings – known in the jargon as the replacement ratio. David Piachaud, of the Centre for Labour Economics at the London School of Economics, has calculated Britain's replacement ratio against an average for eleven other countries. He found that an unemployed single person in the UK gets just 29 per cent of earnings, against an average 58 per cent in the other countries, while for a couple with two children the gap narrows so that in the UK that family gets 52 per cent rather than a 69 per cent average elsewhere.[17]

Making these sorts of comparison is acknowledged to be tricky, because of different countries' uses of flat and earnings-related systems, but the *Economist* newspaper has published figures, based on data drawn from the OECD in Paris, the UK's Department of Health and Social Security and the Centre for Labour Economics, that seem revealing. Denmark tops the league, with about 90 per cent of gross earnings, followed by Holland where 80 per cent at first drops to 75 per cent after six months. France averages about 70 per cent, followed by West Germany where 68 per cent falls to 58 per cent after a year, while Belgium has an indefinite 60 per cent. Ireland's flat-rate system gives a couple with two children 60 per cent of the average breadwinner's gross wage, while the same UK family gets 66 per cent on the combination of the flat rate and the earnings-related system that is being phased out, but only 52 per cent on the flat rate alone.[18]

If producing straightforward arithmetical comparisons is liable to be misleading, because of the fringe benefits of different social security and welfare systems, evaluating the effects of dole payments is largely unexplored territory. But it is most important for governments to set benefits at a level where they do not act as magnets to unemployment, and, with the best will in the world it is no easy task. There are conflicting experiences. In early 1981, the UK Policy Studies Institute published a report – separate from the survey mentioned earlier – suggesting that the higher the benefits paid to the unemployed, the more determinedly they seek work. It all boiled down to the fact that those with high benefits had large families and therefore found it harder to manage, so they were pushed into considering almost any kind of job.[19] But in the US, for local reasons, the reverse often holds true. Because of the means-tested welfare system, notably the Medicaid health care system granted to families below the poverty line, the temptation for the comparatively ill paid is either to drop their earnings or become unemployed to qualify. A misfortune such as a child falling sick can prompt a breadwinner to turn scrounger.[20]

So far, it does not appear that such finely calculated considerations have figured very largely in governments' thinking on unemployment benefits. That is, no doubt, because until now there has been no major shake-out of the jobs market, so that the expense of paying benefits has been tolerable. Now the US government, for instance, has woken up to the fact that each percentage point rise in the unemployment rate will cost an additional $25 billion in federal spending. But the goal still seems to be across-the-board savings on welfare outlay rather than any re-evaluation of the system itself, and that goes for West Germany too where sharp cutbacks are anticipated.

Scrounging is once more the key, according to political analysts like Professor Max Kaase of Mannheim University. In what
looks like a classic two-fisted attack on the issue, the Bonn
government has defused political concern over rising unemployment by stressing that West Germany's jobless level is
considerably lower than the rates in neighbouring European
countries. And at the same time it has made it plain that a
reduction in the Federal Republic's budget deficit is the top
priority, leaving little room for doubt that unemployment benefit
will have to bear its share of the cutbacks. That a good proportion of the registered unemployed are perceived as spongers,
says Kaase, makes benefit reductions politically possible, while
the fact that foreign 'guestworkers', young people and women,
all sections of society lacking political weight, will be first hit
helps explain the lack of controversy to date.

In the US the conservative tide that swept Ronald Reagan into
the White House makes the pressures on benefits appear irresist-
ible. American liberals fear that the present mood of comfort-
able middle-class selfishness, that is unmoved by the plight of
the poor, bodes extremely ill for the country. In contrast to
Kennedy's 'New Frontier' and Johnson's 'Great Society' or
the Nixon-Ford-Carter years of the 1970s when progressive
policies created 18 million new jobs, the Reagan administration
is charged by its critics with embarking on a course that will turn
the industrial cities of the north east and mid-west from areas in
serious decline into social wildernesses. In all fairness, there is
probably some room for reform, such as the system under which
a favoured few industrial workers – thanks to company sponsored benefit schemes negotiated by the unions back in the
mid-1950s, when it must all have seemed a bit remote – can get up
to 90 per cent of their wage earnings when on the dole.[21] But for
most of America's unemployed, benefits and welfare programmes are no gravy train.

The first item in America's complicated benefits system to go
under the axe is the Trade Adjustment Assistance for workers
made redundant by import penetration, which for 1981 is likely

to cost $2·7 billion but in 1982 could be whittled down to $350 million. Then the Reagan administration has turned to unemployment benefits themselves. These are operated under a cumbersome 'hybrid' system in which the 50 states pay the first six months from their own taxes and the federal government takes over thereafter or, as now, when the US national unemployment rate tops 4·5 per cent. It wants, instead, a system of state 'triggers' so as to avoid Washington shouldering the burden of benefits in states where unemployment is still below the national 4·5 per cent trigger rate.[22]

But it is not these details that are creating the most anxiety, nor even the Reaganites' draconian plan for forcing anyone unemployed for more than three months to take the first job offered, providing it pays the minimum wage of just over three dollars an hour. It is the cuts in federal welfare spending that will slice into aid to the poor providing food, housing and heating. Although President Reagan had originally promised that none of his administration's budget cuts would hurt the 'truly needy', his critics claim that 660,000 families in the US with incomes below the poverty line of about $8500 a year will be all but denied welfare aid.[23]

The administration's bid to trim $1·8 billion from the $11 billion federal food stamps programme, for instance, means that the 22 million Americans who now receive the subsidy will see it cut by an average of 10 per cent. According to an estimate in the *New York Times*, a mother of two on welfare loses about $300 a year on food stamps, while other cuts will cost her $400 a year more through reductions in health subsidies and emergency assistance for fuel bills. The newspaper cited an Ohio family 'struggling to survive' on the present rate of $142 a month in food stamps plus $263 in welfare.[24]

The newspaper also quoted a local welfare official as saying that, even uncut, food stamps do not buy enough to cover the family's nutritional needs. However, it is just such hard luck stories from the industrial heartland of the world's richest nation that can prompt a nagging doubt. Can families really survive on so little money, or do they sometimes have a supplementary income? A clue lies half buried in that *New York Times* story describing the plight of a redundant Ohio machinist and his family. 'Their utilities', it read, 'have already been shut off once this winter, and sometimes they beg scrap metal from neighbours to sell to junkyards.' The coincidence of an out-of-work metal worker engaged in dealing in metal may be just that, but clearly, even if only in a limited fashion, he is profiting from the 'black economy'.

In the US it tends to be called the underground economy, and experts almost all agree that it is now growing very fast indeed. Poor people's 'survival strategies', according to Edgar L. Feige at the University of Wisconsin, now have a 'cumulative impact' equal to a staggering 27 per cent of the US gross national product. Guesstimating illegally undeclared, tax-avoiding work is naturally far from easy, but that figure still seems very high. More credible is the assessment of another American economist, Professor Peter M. Gutmann of the City University of New York. He puts what he calls 'the subterranean economy' in the US at about $220 billion, or ten per cent of GNP. Estimates by the US Internal Revenue Service, which after all has more than a passing interest in the subject, place the size of the underground economy at somewhere between 5·9 and 7·9 per cent of GNP. The IRS reckons that some 15 million to 20 million Americans fail to declare income worth several hundred billion dollars and that 4·5 million people live entirely on earnings from unofficial jobs.

The size of these black economies is important. Not so much because governments are determined to clamp down on them and staunch lost tax revenues they know are leaking away, but because they provide a means of work and support when jobs in the formal economy are evaporating.

Italy, rather than America, is generally thought to have far and away the largest black economy of any industrialized country, with about twenty per cent of the GNP undeclared and off the books,[25] and almost a third of Italian exports produced in areas where labour is undeclared. It is tempting for Italians and others to justify it all by saying that what cannot be counted by official-dom does not harm anyone, and indeed that the absence of bureaucratic meddling probably stimulates business. But the darkest side of Italy's black economy is rising and illegal use of child labour, possibly as many as half a million children, some as young as nine, in a trade that the London Anti-Slavery Society has described to the United Nations as under 'Mafia-type control'.[26]

In all, there are reckoned to be 3 million to 5 million Italian workers engaged in 'lavoro nero', considerably more than the 1·8 million registered unemployed although there is certainly some overlap between the two categories.

Other European countries also have thriving black economies, if not on the same scale. In Britain the number of undeclared workers is estimated at 2·3 million, with undeclared income in 1978–9 reckoned by the Inland Revenue at about £11 billion, or 7·5 per cent of GNP. One useful guide to the growth in undeclared income is said to be the increase between 1972 and 1978 in the volume of £10 and £20 notes in circulation – they rose by 470 per cent, which not even the country's wayward money supply figures can account for. In West Germany 'Schwarzarbeit' is thought to have grown fivefold in as many years, with 2 million workers accounting for a hidden two per cent of GNP. In France about 1 million people are engaged in a fairly small black economy that has been whittled down by officialdom to the size of the country's motor industry.

All in all, there are thought to be about 16 million unregistered workers in the 24 'rich' countries grouped in the OECD, and the extent to which those are the same faces that show up in the OECD's 23 million-plus registered unemployed is anyone's guess. But leaving aside governments' and honest taxpayers' understandably resentful views on the whole matter, the important question would seem to be whether these black economies are providing work for the unemployed, which broadly speaking would be a good thing, or whether they are dominated by those who are already employed? The arguments either way are at best inconclusive, with some experts pointing out that the unemployed are often the least well equipped to take advantage of the growth in underground work, because so many of them are unskilled and cannot therefore compete with skilled moonlighters.

The counter-argument is that more and more skilled people have been losing their jobs just as unregistered work has really begun to boom, and that anyway the unemployed have the most marketable commodity of all in the form of almost unlimited free time. Some Belgian observers even complain that their country's tough rules requiring the unemployed to register daily at a time fixed only 24 hours in advance is inhibiting the development of a healthy black market in work that could otherwise be taking up some of the economic slack.

The future of the informal economy is beginning to attract a good deal of academic reflection on both sides of the Atlantic, although so far with rather hazy results. It is one thing to study the more obvious advantages, notably the outlet provided for unused skills and energy and the safety valve for stress and loss of role and identity among the unemployed. But it is quite another to turn it into a legal and fair economy open to all. Besides, underground labour markets are not necessarily in the employees' interest, as any illegal Mexican labourer in the citrus orchards of southern California or North African without correct papers in a Paris sweatshop would attest.

But the informal economy need not be illegal, and perhaps the most promising avenue along which it could progress is that of self-help organizations. The increase in informal co-operatives, created sometimes by groups of redundant workers or promoted by social or educational institutions, is a trend that the European Commission in Brussels is now giving its backing to. Karen Fogg, a senior social affairs official there, emphasizes that self-help ventures providing a range of social and educational services can take on a dynamic of their own and tackle inner-city blight. 'The conventional wisdom on attacking Third World poverty, that of creating a low grade supply/demand economy from the bottom up', she says, 'is as relevant to central Liverpool as it is to the Tanzanian bush.'

It also has the decided advantage of being directly applicable to the undoubted victims of the jobs crisis – women and young people. A few diehards may still cling to notions of the youthful layabout and women who do not 'need' jobs, but the savage speed with which unemployment has reduced them to second class citizenship is now a matter of grave concern. From university graduates to semi-literate black teenagers, the youthful under-25s now account for about half of all the unemployed in the OECD countries. If young men and women have discovered that the labour market is surrounded by no-entry signs, working women of all ages have found themselves being pushed toward the exits. In the European Community, the year up to mid-1981 produced a 25 per cent increase in the number of unemployed women, the US problem has if anything been worse, with women accounting for two-thirds of America's rising unemployment, and in Japan the anyway somewhat suspect jobless total of 1·3 million would be twice that if women had not in recent years been discouraged into simply giving up and going home. It is a sudden and alarming reverse of the trend in which a woman born in 1950 was likely to have a working life of fifteen years, while a girl born in 1970 had until lately been forecast to enjoy 25 years of work.[27]

The idea of people who 'need' to work and others who can get by without formal employment and all that goes with it – cash, friendships and a means of measuring oneself against other people – is an interesting one. It may be that societies will adopt some approach along those lines, but first they would need to identify those people who do not need to work. There do not seem to be many of them. Young people most probably should work, otherwise they do not become integrated into a society that is based on work and their alienation either turns them into social cripples or political revolutionaries. In any case, they mostly want to work. A survey of young people in Britain not long ago were asked the question: 'If you had a private income and did not need to go out to work to make a living, would you still work or not?' Nearly three-quarters, evenly made up of men and women, said they would still wish to work, and amongst the teenagers the proportion was higher still.[28]

On any equitable basis, women as a group are hard to weed out from those who need to work. In the lower-income ranges they need the money, in the higher social reaches of industrialized countries they have during the post-war years gained an average of about 40 per cent of university places, and are conditioned to compete for careers.

People in work but nearing retirement age are increasingly seen as a group that can be displaced by early retirement to make room in the labour market for others 'who deserve a chance'. The trend in Europe's ailing traditional industries has of late been to buy them out to reduce overcapacity. But there are signs that these people nearing the end of their working lives are the least willing to give up their need for work. A 1978 survey of employed people in Britain by National Opinion Polls found that 82 per cent of those close to retirement would not opt to give up work, even if they still received full pay.

The same survey also provoked some illuminating replies from people about their attitude to work. Asked if they enjoyed it a little, a lot or not at all, three-quarters said they liked it a lot.[29]

Perhaps the most puzzling thing of all in the welter of confusing attitudes to work and unemployment, to desirable social security and to scrounging, is the fact that joblessness has already become one of the most widely shared human experiences – not just in the Third World, where very imprecise calculations put unemployment at around 500 million, so that more or less everyone has a member of their immediate family without a livelihood, but in the industrial world too. Back in 1979, before the jobs crisis had begun to bite hard, the European Commission surveyed 9000 Europeans and found that almost half, during a three year period, had personal experience of unemployment. Broken down, it turned out that during the comparatively buoyant years of 1975–8, thirteen per cent of all those interviewed had themselves been unemployed and a further 36 per cent had known a victim of unemployment within their immediate circle. For Europeans under the age of 30, that personal experience of unemployment rose to two-thirds.

At a rough projection, by 1985 those figures will be even more striking. Over a third of all Europeans will on average have themselves experienced unemployment while about half of that third will actually be unemployed, and around 80 per cent or more will have had experience through friends or family of the jobs crisis. Society has yet to think through a fresh and coherent approach to joblessness, but, like hanging, the prospect of experiencing it will no doubt concentrate the mind wonderfully.

Politics and Violence:
the Critical Threshold

President Pompidou of France used to reckon that half a million jobless would be the plimsoll line for social unrest and a return to the revolutionary climate of *les événements de Mai* in 1968.[1] In Britain during the early 1970s when the waters of unemployment were already creeping menacingly up the hull, the figure of 1 million jobless was widely regarded as the danger mark. Since then, political tolerance of unemployment has been observed at first with disbelief and then with something akin to complacency. As the TUC's General Secretary Len Murray caustically observed: 'The employed find it fairly easy to tolerate the unemployment rates.'[2]

Events in British cities during the summer of 1981 have shattered that complacency. For the first time since the 1930s, British workers – albeit youthful 'would be' workers – clashed violently with the police without the complicating alibi of race rioting being immediately available. That it was white and black youths who together attacked a Manchester police station in early July escaped few observers.

The violence that spread through Liverpool, Birmingham, Manchester, Hull and London also made it plain that national unemployment rates are not a sensitive guide to political trouble; it is the local 'critical threshold' of deprivation that encompasses joblessness, poor housing and police methods that counts. It was in fact France, not Britain, that made the discovery. For it was at the odd hour of 5.45 a.m. on a bitterly cold February morning in 1979 that the unemployed in Europe actually cast the first stones. As the night shift came off duty at the threatened Usinor steelworks at Longwy in eastern France, the men chose not to return to their homes but instead gravitated along with the incoming shift toward the bulk of the police Commissariat. Their tense mood quickly turned ugly, and a barrage of missiles exploded against the building. In the days which followed the hard hit Lorraine region erupted into violence.

If the British rioters' frontal assault on such a bastion of civil authority as a Manchester police station took the country by surprise – prompting a stunned William Whitelaw, the Home Secretary, to discuss openly the use of water cannon, rubber bullets and troops hitherto reserved for Ulster – French reaction had been equally shocked.

Although French politics have long had a tradition of voicing protest through random street demonstrations, the *descente dans la rue* that unless gravely mishandled is a salutory way for French militants to let off steam, attacking a police barracks was something different. To the Paris authorities, the Longwy rioting had all the hallmarks of a popular insurrection. Even more alarming was the list of potential flashpoints around France, for there was open speculation that the distressed Lille-Roubaix-Tourçoing textiles and engineering belt in the north could shortly rise to join forces with the former workers of the Saint Nazaire shipyards in the west, leaving only the Lyon and Saint Etienne industrial areas to the south to complete the encirclement of the capital.[3]

In a rash of disobedience similar to that in Britain two years later, events in eastern France moved fast. The spectacle of goods trains forcibly held up, public records publicly burned, endless skirmishes with riot police, the invasion of the Eiffel Tower and a mass march on Paris, was not lost on neighbouring European countries with similar industrial problems.

In terms of revolution, of course, the Longwy violence like its British counterparts turned out to be a damp squib. However much newspapers and television may talk of revolt, political change is a longer and infinitely more complex political process. Looking back on Longwy, not only did it fail to ignite fuses elsewhere, it even failed to save more than 300 of the 7000 suppressed steel jobs that started it all.

But one should not forget that it was the *former* French government that settled comfortably back to its fight against inflation rather than unemployment, once the troubles in Lorraine had died down. Amongst the politicians now best qualified to discuss the political effects of high unemployment can be numbered France's ex-President Valery Giscard d'Estaing and his Prime Minister Raymond Barre. Yet another is one-term President of the United States, Jimmy Carter. In the two Common Market countries with by far the highest joblessness rates, Ireland and Belgium, the views of ousted premiers Charles Haughey and Wilfried Martens might also be instructive.

Heads of government fallen victim to resentments against rising unemployment still form a fairly select club, but it is growing fast. It is a club which will have no prejudice against women members, when the day comes. One of its next members is widely expected to be Margaret Thatcher, judging by the private and public views of her own Cabinet colleagues, let alone those expressed elsewhere.

Senior Tory Party figures predict that the next General Election in the UK in 1983 or '84 is almost certain to be lost in the unusually high number of marginal constituencies to be found in the depressed West Midlands. Other political analysts, though, think that still paints an unrealistically optimistic picture. They believe that if the country's unemployment total is by polling day headed towards the 4 million mark – and if the Thatcher government's unbending attitude to the jobs crisis is perceived to be still unchanged – then it could lose in a landslide, whatever the state of the other political parties.

There is a good argument, though, that such changes in the fortunes of politicians inside the framework of democracy are positively healthy signs. For the risk is that unemployment is becoming so socially divisive that it could breed anti-democratic political developments.

Not that any but the tiniest and most insignificant minority of people would ever deliberately set out to subvert the democratic process or assault it frontally like some Italian *Brigate Rosse* or German *Rote Armee Fraktion*. It is, rather, that the pressures of mass unemployment are becoming such that it is increasingly unlikely that Europe's political landscape will be unchanged by the second half of the 1980s.

Consider the following elements in the social mix that makes up Europe's various but very similar democratic systems. And reflect, too, on whether they are each potentially volatile enough to form a catalyst for sudden political change or to react together to product an explosive mixture.

– By 1986, as many as 60 per cent of an EEC dole queue that could well number 15 million registered unemployed will notionally be under the age of 28 and will never have held a permanent full-time job in their lives. According to sociologists and political analysts, this phenomenon – which was only briefly observable towards the end of the 1930s when fascist-communist street fighting in London's East End was commonplace – is liable to produce a social and therefore political disaffection that is beyond post-war experience.

– Polls conducted in recent years amongst the young in Britain identify clearly two separate trends. The first is a worryingly high tolerance of violence as an acceptable means of settling political issues – a Market & Opinion Research International (MORI) survey of 15–24 year olds in August 1979 found that nearly a third condoned the use of violence to bring about social change. The second is disaffection amongst the young with Britain's two main political parties and the accelerating tendency to vote for alternative and centrist parties.

– Racial minorities and immigrant 'sub-societies' that have not been absorbed into their host countries have become potent forces for de-stabilization. They provide a focus for white discontent over unemployment – even though it is those minorities who have borne the brunt of the jobs shortage – and risk being the root of an increasing number of race riots that are the symptom of competition for work. Europe's immigrant population is made especially volatile not only by years of under-privilege, but also because of its youth. Of Britain's half a million-strong West Indian community, for instance, 80 per cent is currently under 30 years old, as against a national average of 30 per cent.[4]

These three elements, with their common denominator of youth, form the core of political change. And while disaffected youth may represent only a comparatively small proportion of Western Europe's 400 million population, it is the reactions to their anti-social behaviour that would start to upset the political applecarts.

Before looking in detail at the ways in which Europe's politics are susceptible to unexpected change, it would therefore be useful to examine the twin problems of youth and colour and assess what degree of trouble lies in store – not just in Britain, where Manpower Services Commission chiefs like Graham Reid say that the youth unemployment problem 'hasn't even begun to get nasty yet', but in France, West Germany, Holland, Belgium and Italy.

In all those countries, coloured immigrant workers are becoming scapegoats for ills ranging from joblessness to inadequate housing and from rising crime to deterioration in education. With Western Europe's highly visible immigrant workforce now estimated at 7·5 million with a further 6 million dependants, there is plenty of scope for tension. In West Germany the tensions between the indigenous population and the country's 4·5 million resident foreigners have produced warnings of a 'social time bomb',[5] and in France vigilante-style terrorism of immigrants has even been condoned by the Communist Party politicians.[6]

In Belgium there have been sporadic attacks against the foreign community that accounts for ten per cent of the population, with assassinations of North African workers routinely described as 'fascist'.[7] In Italy, where racial tension is a novelty, the leading social affairs institute Censis has estimated that half the 400,000 foreign workers are illegal and, in response to charges that they are responsible for increasing crime and violence, the authorities in 1980 introduced a clampdown on immigration.[8]

Britain's racial tensions nevertheless appear not only the most dramatic but also the most closely related to the unemployment crisis. The spread of rioting in the summer of 1981, even before the Brixton riots in London that spring had been fully analysed by Lord Scarman's inquiry, can have come as no surprise to James Prior, then Secretary of State for Employment. In early June, just a month before sustained rioting broke out across the Midlands, he commented that, if serious social unrest were to occur again, it could well be in the West Midlands. It was an area, he said, that presented the government with much the most difficult problem in terms of unrest because it had never before suffered high unemployment.[9]

Not all Cabinet ministers in the Thatcher government so clearly link unemployment and violence. It is tempting to describe such outbreaks as a 'race riot' that can then be blamed on hooliganism. And because the causes of such rioting are indeed very complex it would take a rash man to single out unemployment alone. The signs are, though, that unemployment and associated deprivations form the bulk of the explosive charge, with police harassment, itself a direct result of those conditions, eventually providing the detonator.

In America's summer of 1967, when civil disorders swept through twenty major US cities in an orgy of rioting and looting that cost at least $100 million in property damage, those were the self same causes.

Those were the findings in the report of the National Advisory Commission on Civil Disorders set up in the aftermath by President Lyndon Johnson. It listed 'police practices' as the primary trigger, ranked high unemployment, particularly amongst blacks, as the second cause, and inadequate housing as the third. In what must rank as one of the most penetrating official X-ray pictures ever taken of urban ghetto life and its woes, it listed the economic, educational, social and political discriminations that had pushed America's non-white urban poor not just outside the structure of society but into open conflict with armed troops.[10]

The US riot commission's catalogue of pressures that had built up inside the ghettoes – and which many Americans believe are again building – would strike an unpleasantly familiar chord with any social workers familiar with, say, West Berlin's Kreuzberg district peopled by Turkish workers, the Paris suburb of Vitry-sur-Seine where the 'bidonville' housing of North African workers has lately sparked racial violence, or the Handsworth district of Birmingham where the minority population is predominantly West Indian.

There is even a depressing déjà-vu in the police activities that sparked the violence of Brixton 1981 and, for example, Detroit 1967. In the case of Brixton it was the spectacle of policemen putting a wounded black youth into their car at a time when repressive tactics to combat crime were being used. In Detroit, similar police methods had been employed for several months, and it was police raids on a number of 'blind pig' illegal drinking joints used by blacks that suddenly provoked spontaneous street violence.

Just to complete the mixture of factors that transform comparatively responsible neighbourhoods into scenes of mob mayhem, there is one other important underlying element, and it makes the problem a good deal more intractable.

It is what some American authorities have called the 'rolling the boulder down the hill' theory. Broadly, it suggests that social upheavals such as massive rioting are more likely to occur in a liberal climate than under conditions of stern repression. When there is an unsympathetic and staunchly conservative Republican administration, wholly prepared to stem trouble with tanks if necessary, it can keep the lid on violence. This is because the discontented recognize that their violence would involve trying to 'roll the boulder up the hill'. But when there is a sympathetic government, such as the Johnson administration that had successfully introduced the 1960s reforms of the 'Great Society', the temptation for the political militants of the ghettoes is to take advantage of the climate to push the authorities into even greater concessions.

Interestingly enough, the Brixton riots took place in the wider context of a considerable relaxation of policing pressure in the area, which suddenly ended with the replacement of the senior police officer by one who had counter-reacted with the rigorous stop-and-search methods of what the police called 'Operation Swamp'. If the 'boulder' theory is correct, the situation surrounding Europe's racial tensions and inner-city blights is greatly complicated. For anything other than an all out effort to meet demands for reform, even before they are made, might conceivably aggravate the problem. In other words, cosmetic attempts by European governments to face-lift conditions in the under-privileged ghettoes might even make matters worse.

That said, it nevertheless appears possible to disarm the detonator of police behaviour in Europe's disadvantaged areas. Intelligent political direction in cities as far removed as Detroit, Michigan, and Birmingham, Warwickshire, has produced two interestingly similar cases. In both, predominantly coloured populations that seemed on the verge of some form of insurrection have been calmed once the police were instructed to reassess their objectives.

Before going into those two examples, it is instructive to glance at the way that society in recent years has been forced to keep the lid on the pressure cooker of the 'have nots' by steadily increasing police strengths out of all proportion to rises in adult population. In France, all police employment has increased by about 25 per cent over the 1970s, while petty theft such as burglary has shot up by 50 per cent. In Britain, where burglary has increased by almost a third over the past ten years and crimes of violence have more than doubled, police strength has gone from 96,000 to almost 120,000. Belgium, with its high unemployment and immigrant levels, has seen armed hold-ups double. Police levels have risen accordingly.

Not to put too fine a point on it, it appears that governments have consistently swept economic and thus social problems under the carpet, and used their police forces to stand on the edges of the carpet to keep things tidy. Yet policing need not be repressive, and indeed seems a good deal more effective when it is not. However, it takes a thorough re-orientation of old attitudes, for as *The Times* pointed out in a perceptive article following the Brixton riots, the police and militant blacks can become locked into a grotesque mirror image of one another. It aptly quoted a senior police officer as saying: 'Don't forget we're a tribe. We're a minority.'[11]

Detroit and Handsworth, where new style policing methods have been paying handsome dividends, are also unlikely mirror images of one another. Detroit has one of America's highest unemployment rates – thanks to the automobile industry's difficulties 250 manufacturing plants out of 1250 have lately disappeared and teenage black unemployment is running at over 60 per cent. At the same time, 'MoTown' Detroit has seen overall crime drop 30 per cent while the US national crime index moves inexorably upwards.[12]

In the mid-1970s, Detroit was notoriously 'Murder City USA' and as a spokesman for the city's police department remarked of those days: 'The more the police had their way, the more they alienated people.' Now the basis of Detroit's counter-attack against crime is organized community involvement in which 3500 'neighbourhood watch' organizations have been set up. It sounds like posse or vigilante tactics, but in fact seems to boil down more to a fresh social proscription of crime. But the message that crime is anti-social, however poor the neighbourhood, also owed much to the police decision to determinedly recruit more blacks in relation to the population of a city that is not only predominantly black but also has had a black mayor since 1974. By 1976 the city had acquired a police chief prepared to state that 'traditional police practices will not reduce crime', and shortly afterwards he introduced a police de-centralization scheme, under which 50 police mini-stations were opened throughout the city and staffed not just by policemen but by 2000 trained volunteers drawn from their local neighbourhoods. In some target districts, assaults and robberies have since dropped by over 60 per cent.[13]

Handsworth, Birmingham, can tell a similar tale, for the West Midlands police force has also moved away from classic tactics of repression to those of much greater community involvement. It did so at a time when the crumbling black ghetto of Handsworth looked ready to explode into violence. According to John Brown, director of the Department of Social Policy at Cranfield Institute of Technology who monitored the situation before the police policy sea-change, public order was threatened. That was in 1977, when he made a special study of the area. But by 1980, following police initiation of moves such as the 'Lozells Project' for providing welfare, education and sporting facilities, John Brown was able to report a marked improvement.

'To revisit Handsworth,' he wrote, 'is to find signs of change. Though unemployment, particularly among young West Indians, continues to rise, sharply in recent times, overall crime levels stay fairly constant; and more significantly street robberies and thefts have notably declined.'[14]

That, together with 'evidence of growing trust and co-operation between police and community', has been no mean feat in an area where teenage unemployment was growing at an annual rate of 134 per cent.[15]

It is also a rare and isolated case, so that for Britain as a whole competition for jobs is building up a head of steam that promises a succession of race riots, although a less misleading term should be coined. For as Ted Knight, leader of Lambeth Council, said immediately after the Brixton disturbances: 'What occurred was not a race riot. It was the police against youngsters who were in the main unemployed, and black in particular.'[16]

In the immediate future, that is to say up to 1985–6, the danger must be that, unless sizeable extra funding is funnelled by central government through to the Manpower Services Commission for the enlargement of the Youth Opportunities Programme, then the levels of teenage unemployment in the UK will reach politically unmanageable proportions. The MSC's internal calculation that school-leavers' unemployment will jump almost tenfold from early 1981 to 1983 – from 78,300 to 700,000 – because existing programmes for keeping them 'off the register' are saturated, has grave implications.[17] As Oscar Hahn, a director of the major Guest, Keen and Nettlefold group that employs 70,000 people, chiefly in the Midlands, submitted not long ago in evidence to the Parliamentary Home Affairs Committee on Race and Immigration: 'There is obviously a threat that this (peace) will not continue if unemployment among the young, particularly the coloured young, continues or even grows. All people are conscious of this.'[18]

Across the Atlantic, Americans are also conscious that their own racial problems are far from solved. Burgeoning unemployment is again at the root of the problem, with the US black population suffering particularly from a 'last in, first out' effect as the decline of manufacturing industry progresses. Having a high proportion of unskilled and, worse, unskilled teenagers ensures that blacks suffer an unemployment rate that is about twice as high as that hitting the white population. But the political trouble is liable to stem most from the fact that skilled black industrial workers are losing their jobs. For from 1940 to the late 1970s American blacks made spectacular progress – even if largely unnoticed – in establishing themselves in manufacturing industry rather than in menial service jobs. During those years the proportion of the black workforce in blue-collar industrial occupation went from 38 per cent to about 60 per cent. But those jobs have been disappearing fast, so that America is now taking away the gains so recently achieved. Whites, meanwhile, dominate the more secure professional, managerial and administrative jobs so that among men four out of ten hold those white collar-plus occupations, while for blacks the figure is only twelve per cent.[19]

The more likely cause of fresh eruptions of black violence, though, is the tough competition for work coming from America's fast growing hispanic population. By the late 1990s the hispanics are due to overtake the blacks to become America's single largest minority, and in the meantime are proving to be hard-to-beat rivals for available work. Professor Michael Piore at the Massachusetts Institute of Technology explains that not the least of their advantages is that Central American immigrants are often comparatively well educated and also tend to have a strong family and social base.

There seems little doubt that this growing black-hispanic rivalry was a major cause of the savage rioting in 1980 in Miami, Florida, and there are understandably fears that further violent clashes are inevitable. The chances are that the Reagan administration's commitment to cutting back on welfare and job support programmes funded by the federal government will exacerbate tensions. Some observers have even speculated that reductions in federal spending on America's under-privileged could have such an impact on the faltering economies of the black ghettoes that their inhabitants would quite literally be starved out on to the highways in search of a livelihood, if not a job, elsewhere. The spectre of a new generation of 'Okies', the dispossessed dust-bowl farmers of the 1930s who were forced to flee the mid-West, conjures up powerful folk memories in America. Other experts, such as Piore, nevertheless believe that as the inner cities fester, their inhabitants will become even more immobile and cut off from the mainstream of society. The choice seems to be between sprinkling the gunpowder around or leaving it concentrated in a few powder kegs.

Perhaps the real danger for America, and a growing one for many European countries, is that the political system provides no mechanism for correcting iniquities. American blacks have no political focus, for national leadership of the civil rights and voter registration movements seems to have died with Martin Luther King, and strongly liberal sympathisers admit that the political Left in the US has never been more bankrupt. At the same time, a voting turnout in the 1980 presidential elections of a shade over half the electorate points to massive alienation of the American people from democracy.

How effective the US minorities' political clout, either 'up on the hill' in Congress, or at state and local level, will prove to be during this century remains to be seen. What is not in doubt is that it is certain, weak though it may be, to be a good deal more muscular than the political influence of the various racial minorities in Europe.

The real question in Europe, though, is not what are the consequences of such widespread abstention from voting, but rather what effect will worsening unemployment have on voting patterns? For to date discontent has shown little sign of deflecting people away from polling even if activists sometimes cheerfully opt for both the ballot and the bullet. West German politicians, for instance, have reportedly become increasingly concerned that large scale civil disobedience is beginning to threaten the democratic system.[20] Militant youth demonstrations in defiance of the law and the police over issues such as squatting rights in empty houses and nuclear power station construction have become rallying points for protestors in their tens of thousands. The same movement has also swept through Holland and into tidy, law-abiding Switzerland. Yet West Germany has an 83 per cent voting turnout, and in the Netherlands the figure is 95 per cent.

European youths' complaints are much more likely to be expressed through using rather than overturning the use of the democratic process, whatever the wishes of the small handful of 'terrorists' allegedly still at the bottom of Germany's student unrest. Throughout the 1970s, the trend has already been for the under-25s to create and support new splinter political parties, notably the ecologist 'Greens' in Germany, while withdrawing their support from the older and established ones.

Some outside observers still fear that during the 1980s the phenomenon of high and sustained youth unemployment will drive young voters into the arms of political extremists. The former US Ambassador to Britain, Kingman Brewster, has warned: 'There is a danger that there will be an urban generation that has never worked and could fall prey to real extremism of the very far Left or the very far Right.'[21]

The possibility of a Britain of the near future, riven by running street battles between the National Front or some other neo-fascist group and militant communists in all their categories, is not something to be ignored. But political analysts like Ivor Crewe at the University of Essex believe that the importance of small extremist organizations can easily be overrated. Of the National Front, he comments: 'It all depends whether you are holding a telescope to the British electorate, or just a microscope.' Its electoral support seems glued at 0·1 per cent.[22]

Europe's post-war history suggests that lurches toward extremism in democratic countries only become a real risk when it is virtually impossible for the electorate to remove the government in power and replace it with a genuine alternative. People may sometimes complain of the 'Buggins' turn' way in which governments of the Left and the Right not only succeed each other but reverse each other's policies, yet it seems to be a remarkably effective safety valve. In West Germany it is thought no accident that the heyday of neo-Nazism occurred in 1968–9 when the Christian Democrats and the Social Democrats were in unholy, and for a while seemingly unbudgeable, coalition. In France the excesses of May '68 coincided with a widespread feeling that Gaullism had gained a monolithic control of government. In Italy, a country where rather less importance is attached to the process of government than is usual, the indefinite lease on power taken by the Christian Democrats has helped spawn the terrorism of the Red Brigades.

The real mistake that Giscard made, one his supporters only half-jokingly remarked after the French President had failed to win re-election in May, 1981, was to give the vote to the 18-year olds. It is also reckoned that Francois Mitterand's ability to 'rejuvenate' France's Socialist Party – in contrast to the apparently unchanged nature of the Communist Party – ensured the success of his appeal to the vital youth vote.

Where that same political power of the under-30s will affect West Germany and Britain is a good deal less clear, although in Germany at any rate the chances of any resurgence of Right-wing extremism seem very remote. According to a poll commissioned by Chancellor Helmut Schmidt's office in Bonn, only four per cent of the 18–21 age group showed any support for neo-Nazi views. The bulk of the overall thirteen per cent of the electorate, a total of 5·5 million people, who did subscribe to militant Right-wing policies were over 50-years old. More worrying, perhaps, were the findings of another poll in West Germany at about the same time that attempted to plumb the political opinions of the country's 1 million students. Its findings suggested that half reject many of the present social values and tend to opt somewhat incoherently for an 'alternative' society devoid of pressures and material values and firmly against all things nuclear or military. The predominant factor shared by youth over the age of fourteen was apathy, with only three per cent seeing themselves as 'activists' in any political sense.[23]

In Britain, reading the political runes is a good deal more perplexing. Psephologists, pollsters and political geographers have only slowly been coming to grips with the fact that the nature of UK unemployment has changed – so that instead of being a misleading 'snapshot' of people in between jobs it is increasingly a structural problem with a real political impact. Yet they have been aware that, not far beneath the surface of what one might call Britain's 'tidal' two party system, some very interesting developments have lately been taking place. It is beginning to look as if youthful voters are scrapping the traditional 'class' attachments to either of the major parties, and, irrespective of their backgrounds or occupations, are being drawn toward the untried Centrist alternatives of the Liberals or the new Social Democrats.

Michael Steed of Manchester University, a leading analyst of voting patterns, believes that the Liberals and the SDP can now count on very strong youth support, with the Social Democrats even exerting an appeal to voters aged up to 40 years old. Labour's appeal to youth he estimates to be waning. Backing up his assertions, for Steed himself has strong Liberal Party connections, an independent opinion poll conducted by MORI in early 1981 on behalf of the *New Statesman* magazine, found that the

Liberals rather than Labour will be the beneficiaries of discontent over high unemployment. The survey of course pre-dated the setting up of the SDP, but it did establish that 'the most discernible shift is towards the Liberals'. In an analysis of the poll, Peter Kellner of the *New Statesman* commented, 'This is bad news for Labour. At a time when unemployment is soaring, the major opposition party is failing to pick up extra support among the worst victims of the government's economic policies.'[24]

Politicians seldom tire of pointing out that the only opinion polls that really count are elections, and, given that that MORI survey offered little encouragement to Labour and none to the Conservatives, the bulk of the House of Commons would probably wish to fall back on that answer. But a look back over the 1970s makes it all too plain that Britain's younger voters have largely abandoned old class loyalties to the two main parties, and have instead become a highly critical floating vote with a major influence on the outcome of elections. The young have historically been more volatile than their elders, but, if their links with the major parties are now so tenuous that in the next General Election many of them vote for neither, the outcome could be a sea-change in British Politics. Robert Worcester, who heads MORI, also points out that support for the SDP appears to be a close reflection of the population profile. 'It is not a middle-class, middle-aged party as some have suggested.'[25]

In the May 1979 election that brought Mrs Thatcher to power, the young, the skilled working class and women were three dominant factors that contributed to the outcome. And in comparison to the previous October 1974 General Election they, together with trade union members, transferred their allegiances in most disconcerting fashion. Labour lost much of its traditional support among the skilled working class that makes up a third of the electorate and is an obvious and vital part of the party's vote. Not only did it lose them, it lost them so heavily that they swung 11·5 per cent to the Tories, which was double the rate of swing that gave Mrs Thatcher her victory. The Conservatives also doubled their youth vote, getting 42 per cent rather than the 24 per cent youth vote they had previously held. They did so at the expense of the Liberals, whose youth vote was halved to just twelve per cent, but they also picked up substantially from the 18–24 year old mainly first time voters who usually vote Labour if they vote at all.[26]

For a further element that muddies the waters of Britain's voting behaviour is that inside electoral turnout rates that have averaged 75 per cent of all available votes over the last twenty years, youth voting turnouts have been falling. Michael Steed attributes this to the 'non-efficacious' character of voting in Britain's first-past-the-post system, by which he means not so much the lack of proportional representation but the absence of a preliminary round of voting such as in France that encourages candidates to modify policy stances in the light of first round voting. But, as the British system is most unlikely to be changed to resemble that of France, the question most relevant to the increasingly volatile youth vote is whether the despair of unemployment could discourage the jobless young men from voting at all and so reduce their clout when Mrs Thatcher goes to the country.

Youth that does not vote almost certainly includes a high proportion of the deprived, ill-educated, socially alienated and politically illiterate who are the core of the worsening urban violence. The idea that the rather less underprivileged will react to rising unemployment with massive abstentions does not seem very plausible. More likely they will exact revenge at the polls.

Some commentators see Britain increasingly divided into 'two political nations',[27] judging by the May 1981 county council elections that virtually drew a line from the Wash to the Bristol Channel with Labour's writ running to the north of that and that of the Tories, and to some extent of the Liberals, to the south. Others have looked at the region by region forecasts of the growth of unemployment up to 1985 – notably a recent study by the Warwick University Manpower Research Group – and concluded that much of the job losses still to come will strike at the heartland of Tory support. Unemployment in the south east and south west, for instance, is predicted to double between 1980 and 1985, going from just over five per cent to 10·4 per cent.[28]

Guessing at the outcome of Britain's next General Election would be foolhardy in the present state of flux, although it is tempting to speculate that the 1980s could produce some flimsy coalitions of the centre. What does seem certain is that, if the unemployed rise to close on 5 million by the mid-80s as some forecasts threaten, so that indirectly at any rate the dole queues reach out to touch almost one household in three, then the politically stable post-war years are now drawing to a close. In essence that was the warning of France's Finance Minister, Jacques Delors, to his ministerial colleagues from 23 other industrialized nations at the mid-1981 council meeting of the OECD.[29]

If unemployment does indeed mean punishment at the polls for successive governments in Britain and elsewhere, it seems odds-on that a fresh strain of political thought will emerge from the chaos. Perhaps the 1990s will have as their hallmark a general political consensus on the division of jobs and wealth, in much the same way as the slump years of the thirties yielded a profound political re-think that gave birth to the Welfare State a decade later and to a bi-partisan goal of full employment.

Turning back to history, though, is as dangerous as it is attractive. There are many pitfalls, the most obvious being that there are now more unemployed in Britain than at any time during the 1930s. For the winter 1932–3 peak of just under 3 million unemployed was almost entirely head of household working men, who represented genuine hardship for tens of millions more. Yet the period exerts a powerful siren call, and at very least its political precedents throw up a range of intriguing questions.

Will, for example, the UK unemployment levels of the 1980s throw up a militant organization comparable to the National Unemployed Workers' Movement (NUWM) of 50 years ago? Could the extreme Left-wing of British politics, from Trotskyites to Bennites, coalesce around such a movement were it to grow out of the May 1981 'People's March for Jobs', and its likely successors? Would such a development once again splinter the Left, in the same way that the communist-dominated NUWM became a threat to the authority of the TUC? Might existing divisions within the leadership of the Labour Party be so exacerbated as to make possible a re-run of Ramsay MacDonald's 'betrayal' of the party by forming the 1931 National Government with the Conservatives, and Labour's subsequent years of eclipse?

For the TUC's continued control of unemployment demonstrations, the writing may already be on the wall. Even though it clearly plans to remain firmly in the saddle while orchestrating a campaign of rallies and sundry protests, it could yet find the initiative wrenched from it by an activist fringe that could exploit Congress House's failures to bring about any radical changes in the Thatcher government's monetarist policies. The seeds of such an out-flanking by the Far Left are already sown. One of the 500-strong core of the May 1981 Jobs March estimated that 'about a fifth of the marchers were communists or belonged to the Socialist Workers' Party and other splinter groups'.[30] The Thatcher government is liable to make matters worse by eroding the TUC's authority, if the remarks in the House of Commons in late May, 1981, by Peter Morrison, Under-Secretary of State for Employment, are any guide. He said that the government was doing everything in its power to alleviate unemployment where possible, but was entitled to ask whether, in a parliamentary democracy, marches were the right way to influence government policy.[31]

With the TUC already smarting and angry at the way the Thatcher government has shut it out of the consultative process in policymaking, that was at best a disingenuous comment. It also chose to ignore the reality that marching is almost the only way to publicise an 'invisible' problem like unemployment. It may well be that during the next few years marches, and the government's decisions on how to handle them, will develop into a 'hearts and minds' propaganda war aimed at winning over the British public.

If so, the Thatcher government will not have the dubious advantage of being able to suppress important elements of media coverage, as was the case with earlier governments' handling of many NUWM hunger marches during the first half of the 1930s.

The chief reason why the famous Jarrow 'Crusade' of 1936 passed into the history books, leaving the much larger and more significant hunger marches of earlier years to be mere footnotes, is that the tiny affair numbering just 200 marchers was a carefully stage-managed exercise in public relations. With the pressures being exerted by the newly founded National Council for Civil Liberties, set up in 1934 to counter the often savage repression of marchers, the authorities were apparently concerned to gain some propaganda advantage. So too was the Labour Party, which rejected NUWM overtures to bolster the demonstration, and so indeed were the Jarrow marchers themselves who did not want their plea for the revitalization of the shipyard to be buried amongst wider political demands. The result was a 'clean' march, untainted by communist involvement, and the authorities took the step of lifting the usual restrictions to allow the newsreel cameras to film it.

When the marchers reached London in early November they were permitted to witness the King, Edward VIII, as he passed along the Mall, and 'showed their enthusiasm by cheering lustily'. They then went to the House of Commons, where they were entertained to tea by sympathetic MPs, and taken on a sight-seeing trip down the Thames. Meanwhile, Jarrow's newly-elected MP and architect of the march, Ellen Wilkinson, presented a petition to 'humbly pray' that work should be provided to a town with 80 per cent male unemployment. A Special Branch report to the Home Office had earlier approved the idea of tea on the terrace at Westminster, on the grounds that 'it would be a good way of encouraging and placating them', and the real victors of the episode became the government which had demonstrated that calm and responsible appeals were the best policy. Even so, no action was taken to aid Jarrow, and in line with the normal practice aimed at deterring marches the men's dole money was docked because they had not been 'available' for work.[32]

The real losers were the NUWM, whose simultaneous rally in Hyde Park attracted up to quarter of a million people and a good deal less publicity.

Judging by the miles of column inches and TV film footage that the Jobs March and inner-city rioting have already chalked up, there is little chance that the politics of unemployment will in this decade lack for intense scrutiny. With the progress over the last 50 years in social attitudes, it is unlikely that the unemployed will have to contend with the same indifference and even antipathy that was sometimes accorded those on the dole by the more fortunate beneficiaries of the 1930s boom industries.

Yet the 'scroungers' debate is far from over, to judge by a report in *The Times*, as the Jobs Marchers neared London, of a Home Counties' pub displaying a 'no marchers' sign.[33] In the same way that Conservative governments may be bolstered or assailed by their own reactionary supporters. Left-wing governments in Europe, such as the new French socialist administration, face even graver domestic political dangers. Perhaps it is the frankness of the post-election honeymoon period, but they freely admit that failure to meet the heightened expectations of the Left on both job-saving and job-creating could well spell double trouble.

As a senior official at the Hotel Matignon, the office of French Premier Pierre Mauroy, remarked of the domestic and international political gambles that unemployment dictates, 'They are the only way to avoid a world war.'[34]

Trade Wars and Worse

Could the 1980s be shaping up for a re-run of the 1930s? The emerging parallels with events of 50 years ago are already uncomfortable. Then, mass unemployment put nations into an uncontrollable tailspin of trade wars and a subsequent arms race that culminated in the onset of world war.

Yet warnings of war are still hard to swallow, even when they have the authority of the Hotel Matignon behind them. France's purpose, though, is to promote concerted international action to tackle the unemployment crisis and defuse the protectionist pressures that risk being such a dominant and dangerous theme in world politics during this decade.

The worry is that trade protectionism could so sour the climate of co-operation between the leading industrial countries, and so destabilize conditions in the newly industrialized and still developing ones, that the odds on there being armed conflict of some kind will soon begin to shorten alarmingly. There are about 30 small wars being fought in the world today, and each is potentially the detonator for a larger explosion.

Prophets are never honoured in their lifetime, and least of all those of doom. But the soothsayers are generally agreed that something will have to give in a world where too many factories are now chasing too few customers. Saturation has become the key word in the highly industrialized countries, for those are the societies in which the workers could afford to buy each other's products and so created the post-war economic boom years. Now the workers are in effect sated. The best example is the motor car, the driving force of industrial expansion. When demand for cars was still unsatisfied, the North American and European markets were being expanded by first-time buyers at a yearly rate of 12–13 per cent and a whole host of other industries were pulled along by that growth. Now consumers mainly only replace their old cars, so the market grows at only 2–3 per cent a year.[1]

Everyone knows that there are plenty of unsatisfied potential consumers left in the world who in theory could set the industrial merry-go-round turning again. Out of the present global population of 4·3 billion, no more than 1 billion could by any stretch of the imagination be said to belong to industrialized, consumer societies. There are plenty more to come, with more than 1 million new people being added to the population every week, so that the increase of about 2 billion over the next twenty years will actually exceed the number of people there were on earth in the years just before World War I.[2]

Equally familiar is the snag: it is that the industrialized countries would need almost to give away their products, which would involve inventing a new system of funding and distributing that would be quite foreign to that of selling and marketing. There is nevertheless a good deal of evidence that priming the pump of Third World demand, both by handing over jobs and goods, can quickly produce more work and wealth for the industrialized countries. A recent study by the UN's International Labour Office in Geneva showed that in 1976 exports by the North (the jargon for the rich countries) to the South (poor Third World ones) were responsible for the creation of 2·4 million new jobs in the North. Imports into the North from the South – such as low-cost textiles – caused the loss of 800,000 Northern jobs, so that there was a net gain of 1·6 million new jobs.[3]

So far, though, the North is a long way from creating a new dynamic for its industries by stimulating demand in the South. It is behaving more like the unscrupulous operator of a company store; the interest of the first week's 'tick' rolls forward and increases, but while it locks the worker into buying from the store it short-sightedly doesn't increase his purchasing power. The

North's trade surplus with the South in manufactured goods is now running at well over $100 billion a year, and is depressing the Third World's ability to buy more.

Far from acknowledging the error of their ways – and heeding warnings such as those of the Brandt Report that new North-South initiatives are urgently needed 'for the survival of mankind' – the industrialized countries are instead setting up the developing countries as the first targets for protectionist action. In the French phrase, it is like 'shooting at ambulances', although it could well turn out to be more like shooting at ammunition wagons. For the developing countries now represent a teetering, ramshackle structure of international debt, which, if weakened by defaults on interest payments at just a few key points, might collapse taking the Western banking system with it. Almost 40 per cent of the outstanding debt of Third World companies is owed to the international capital market in the shape of bank loans and export credit deals, whereas ten years ago it was predominantly money provided on a more stable basis by governments. The cost of servicing that debt, paying interest without reducing the principal sum, for the developing countries other than those in OPEC during the three years up to the end of 1981 is put at $120 billion. A very real problem is that the terms on which much of the money has been borrowed are commercial ones ill-suited to faltering Third World economies – banana republics playing in the multi-national corporations' league. Like the case of the worker in hock to the company store, the problem is getting worse because the debt burden is now growing faster than the Third World borrowers' likely earnings. The World Bank has calculated that, while in 1975–7 the relatively wealthy Third World countries needed to borrow $40 billion a year to keep afloat, by 1985 they will need (in 1979 dollars) something like $155 billion for that year rising to $270 billion for the year 1990. For the really poor countries, aid not loans is already the only answer.

The Third World exports that not only pay for imports from the North but are also needed to service all that debt are now being rapidly overhauled by the size of the debt. In 1977 it was calculated that less than ten per cent of the developing countries' exports had to be set aside to pay interest on their borrowing, although in some poorer countries it had reached twenty per cent. Now it seems that by 1990 that proportion will more than double, so that for each dollar a poor country earns in exports it will only receive 50 cents as the balance goes to the banks. Of course no business could survive under those conditions, and perhaps a better analogy would be that of a poor, debt-ridden family trying to survive on the breadwinner's minimum wage when every year there is an extra mouth to feed. Some experts think it can't go on, but not necessarily all believe that the answer is to give aid or cheaper credit. Henry Wallach, a governor of the US Federal Reserve Board – the American central bank authority – observed recently: 'The US and international banks cannot indefinitely continue funding the less developed countries' (LDCs) deficits. The borrowing countries will have to cut down on their demands for funds.'[4] The trouble is that either way, by lending the Third World more or by lending it less, the industrialized countries in their present 'capitalist' frame of mind will force the South to earn less and thus import and consume less.

To some trades union leaders, and businessmen and workers in industries where jobs are being lost to import competition at an accelerating rate, all this can seem pretty esoteric stuff. They know that their livelihoods are being taken by the cheap labour conditions of the developing world, and they want a stop put to it. Their lobbies are powerful, jobs are votes and so far worried governments in Europe and the US have been 'sympathetic', while conducting rear-guard actions in defence of free trade that seem to acknowledge the eventual victory of protectionism.

Those governments have certainly not to date dared a counter-attack using some of the solid research that shows how most of the jobs being lost are in fact grabbed by one industrialized country at the expense of another. Or how the few jobs being gained by the Third World, as it strives to chip away at an 'official' unemployment of over 60 million people, have really had a negligible effect.

The textile industry is a case in point, for it is widely quoted as a fundamental cause of Europe's rocketing unemployment rates and looks like being the first example in the 1980s of calculated protectionism. It is also directly relevant to the parallel of the 1930s, although more of that later. For the signs are that the new 1982–4 Multi-Fibre Arrangement (MFA) – the North-South textiles trade deal begun in the early 1970s to liberalize conditions and help the developing countries – will be used to deal the Third World a crippling blow. Yet the 1 million jobs that have already been suppressed in the European textiles and clothing industries during the 1970s, bringing the remaining ones down to about 4 million, and the further 2 million at risk during the 1980s, are really a consequence of the major economies of scale available to the EEC's competitors in the US and the state-trading 'Comecon' countries of Eastern Europe. An analysis in London of UK textile trade jobs lost in the five years up to 1975 found that the developing countries' responsibility for all the jobs lost was 0·05 per cent for textile yarn jobs, 0·4 per cent for footwear, 0·8 per cent for cotton fabrics and 1·07 per cent for clothing manufacture.[5] It's not enough to be punished for, and, although it is now thought to be rising, many Third World experts unashamedly wish it were a good deal more because a labour-intensive industry like textiles has a direct drive effect on a weak economy. With the investment cost of each new textiles job in Europe now being put at a quarter of a million dollars, Europeans could arguably spend the money in greater 'added value' sectors and be certain of profits.[6]

The political philosophy of most governments in the industrialized world is still that free trade must be defended. Self-interest alone dictates that, for the prosperous post-war years were marked by an explosion in the volume of world trade. In the 30 years from the late 1940s, international trade grew by a factor of seven and for the industrialized countries, which mainly trade with each other, it was outstripping the handsome increases being made in manufacturing output. Taking 1960 as a starting point, their exports of manufactured goods had doubled in volume by 1967 and by 1972–3 their factories were turning out twice as much as they had been in 1960. It was no coincidence, and by 1976, despite the recession of the first oil shock, the manufactured exports of the developed countries had yet again doubled from their 1967 level. In the early 1970s a high-level group of analysts that had been studying international trade was able to report to the OECD in Paris with quiet satisfaction: 'It is indeed difficult to imagine a greater contrast than that between the period of bilateralism, trade and monetary restrictions, economic stagnation and unemployment that preceded the Second World War, and the postwar period characterized by . . . all-round lowering of trade barriers and unprecedented economic expansion.'[7] Or as a special 'background paper' prepared for British MPs in March 1981 by the Research Division of the House of Commons Library put it: 'Full employment (1945–70) was a consequence of the immense boom in trade between industrial countries.'[8]

But these are lessons that seem to be forgotten as protectionism becomes more and more a 'legitimate' instrument of governments' policies. In political terms, because they have no easy means of retaliation, the Third World countries clearly provide the first easy pickings for the protectionists.

But, as they are not really the job-robbing villains of the piece, erecting high tariff walls and setting low quotas will not actually solve the problem. It will at some point become plain that other countries must also be to blame; and perhaps more so. So who will be next? The NICs – the 'Newly Industrialized Countries', such as Brazil, South Korea, Singapore, Hong Kong and Taiwan? They pose more of a political problem, but yes, they're next. Indeed, they are already being assailed, for in the world textile MFA negotiations at the end of 1981 the industrialized countries singled out Hong Kong, Taiwan and South Korea, which together account for 40 per cent of the low-cost textiles exported by the thirteen major LDC producing nations, as having less of a 'moral right' to the markets of the North than the genuine Third World.

Then comes a dilemma. Assuming that the whole protectionist tide has not already begun to get out of hand – with different states starting unexpectedly and sometimes illogically to declare trade war on one another as they did real war in 1914 – which countries with real muscle do the Western nations then turn on? The trade-troublesome satellites of the Soviet Union, including dangerously unstable Poland, or Japan?

Japan looks a good bet if ever there was one. As one of America's newest economist whizz-kids, Professor Lester Thurow of the Massachusetts Institute of Technology, observes: 'The Japanese are making the world a fundamentally different place to live in. The Europeans are unused to Japanese levels of export competition, and the US is not used to any technological competition at all.'[9] The Japanese are widely believed to be guilty on two counts. Not only are they extraordinarily successful, they are also 'cheating'. They are considered to shut competitors' products out of their own home market, importing just 0·001 per cent of all the cars they export, while at the same time they are accused of resorting to unfair dodges to boost their sales to others.

They are suspected of persistently manipulating the Yen's exchange rate to prevent its value rising and therefore blunting the edge of Japanese export prices. Their non-tariff barriers for refusing entry to foreign goods on technical pretexts are widely cited and their low manufacturing costs, together with the constructive relationship that exists between business, banking and government, are viewed as a form of conspiracy. In Washington not long ago the US perception of Japan's success in international markets was summed-up sourly by an official at the government's General Accounting Office: 'Various forms of government aid to Japanese industry, including tax breaks, cheap credit and restrictions on imports have been the main elements of Japanese competitiveness.' In Brussels, as the Common Market's trade deficit with Japan has roughly doubled year on year of late so that it is now headed for $20 billion a year, the complaint has been that Tokyo refuses to 'open' its markets to Europe.

Fifty years ago, Europeans and Americans were making much the same noises. A glance back at the early 1930s can produce an overwhelming sense of déjà-vu. When G. E. Hubbard published in 1935 his authoritative analysis of Japan's growing industrial might, *Eastern Industrialisation and its Effect on the West*, the gripes were the same then as now. In 1933, despite Britain's frantic recourse to imperial preference protectionist measures, Japan had overtaken the UK as the world's largest exporter of cotton textiles.[10] In what sounds like a present-day analysis of Japan's strategy up to, say, 1970 Hubbard commented of the 1920s: 'Japan was still largely in a state of capital development, building up reserves of capital, productive capacity, and technical and managerial skill. Though that chapter in her evolution cannot be regarded as yet entirely closed, from 1930 onwards the completion of certain parts of her new productive machinery has been returning a dividend in the shape of increased exports of manufactured goods.'

Reaction to Japan's 'enormous expansion in textile exports', a sector at the time as sensitive as motor manufacturing is now, was bitter. The advantages said to be enjoyed by the Japanese included currency depreciation, low manufacturing costs (derived then from cheaper labour rather than high productivity) and a centralized organization of industry that was viewed with the same resentment as Japan Inc. is today.

The Japanese response to these suggestions, that it was 'unfair' tactics that gave its industries such an edge, is striking. In 1934 a Japanese government official observed that in the West 'labour aims at working the shortest possible hours, doing the minimum amount of work and getting the highest possible wage'.[11]

By that time, following the 1931 Ottawa Agreement at which Britain had rallied its empire with a system of tough new protectionist trade preferences, duties on non-British cotton piece goods aimed at pushing Japan out of Asian markets had gone to 50 per cent in 1932 and up to a staggering 75 per cent the following year. Japan's export drive was in fact not stopped in its tracks, although the Japanese military's political influence was considerably enhanced by the sudden onset of protectionism and what was described as the 'encirclement' of Japan by the 'ABCD' powers – Americans, British, Chinese and Dutch. The Ministry of War in Tokyo was by 1934 putting out pamphlets emphasizing the way in which the country was being victimised. 'Countries suffering economic stagnation and anxiety concerning the international situation', ran one, 'are jealous of the Empire's foreign trade expansion and her growing political power.'[12]

Japan's military spending, meanwhile, had become quite alarming. It had risen from an already hefty quarter of all government expenditure in 1931–2 to almost half in 1935–6. Even so, observers like Hubbard took a fairly relaxed view and attributed the surge to the cost of the Manchuria campaign, Japan's foray into China that began in 1931, and to some extent the 'rivalry' between its navy and army.

Japan's war in North China was already being justified as a legitimate search for new trade markets to replace those being closed off to Japanese industry by Western protectionism.[13] And the boom in naval construction was considered in Japan to be a necessary response to what appeared as a threat by the ABCD powers to deny her the use of the traditional oil supply routes from the Middle East, particularly the oil lanes through such vulnerable points as the Straits of Malacca and the openings into the Timor Sea. To most Japanese eyes, almost intolerable economic pressures were shaping the policies that in fact put the country on a war footing. The 1929–32 Great Depression, and the subsequent sharp depreciation of the Yen when Japan was forced off the gold standard, meant massive increases in the price of oil and raw material imports that forced the country into a major exports drive; in much the same way that the 1973 and 1979 oil shocks have done. Japan was also having to contend with a population explosion during the 1930s, so that the Manchurian invasion was characterized as an understandable bid for 'Lebensraum'. Most important of all, of course, was that the antipathy these various actions was creating in the West in turn heightened the mood of pan-Asianism in Tokyo. The seeds of the Greater East Asia Co-Prosperity Sphere, in which Japan 'would lead other Asian nations in liberating themselves from British and American imperialism', were sown.[14]

Looking back, it seems quite clear that, although by the mid-1930s Japan and what were to become 'the Allies' had created the conditions for war, both sides were largely oblivious of the looming hostilities. At any rate, which countries were shaping up against which others was still very fuzzy. In 1936 a senior US industrialist in Tokyo for talks with competitors could say: 'In my view, it is a pity that Japan alone is carrying the fight against communism in Manchuria, and I will go so far as to say that other countries should bear a portion of the costs.'[15]

Protectionist moves against Japan in the 1980s by America and the Europeans have not yet fomented such a pitch of mutual resentment. But it is hard to see how the economic conditions of the 1980s can fail to yield similar tensions, as Japan's industrial strength is once again a serious threat to international political stability. It is reasonable to argue that, even if Japanese companies were deliberately to soft-pedal their export efforts, their products will nevertheless be sucked into a vacuum in European and North American markets produced by the domestic manufacturers' higher costs and technological shortcomings. The point seemed to be made forcibly enough in the autumn of 1980, when I was watching the latest Datsun model roll off the robotized production line at the Nissan works outside Tokyo. The $6000 cars had a computerized control system and digital read-out at that time to be found in Europe only on $30,000 cars such as a BMW. I asked the Nissan executive standing next to me what the export price for European markets had been fixed at. 'You in Europe keep telling us', he said, 'not to export so many cars, so this is being restricted to the domestic market here. But I suppose we shall have to give in to pressure from dealers abroad before too long.'

The imbalance between Japanese industry's capabilities and those of industry in Europe and North America is causing deep concern. A study produced in mid-1981 by European Research Associates, Brussels, into trends toward protectionism in the EEC neatly summarized the basic problem. The non-Atlantic producers have, it commented, 'revealed Europe for what it is – a high-cost area of production almost as quickly rendered uneconomic as European coal was by Arabian oil in the 1950s'. The fear is that not just motor manufacturing, shipbuilding and domestic electronics such as TVs and hi-fi equipment will increasingly be swamped by Japanese producers, but that key industrial products such as numerically controlled machine tools, engineering components and a yet unborn generation of microelectronic equipment will also be dominated by the Japanese at the expense of employment in Europe.

So far tensions over Japanese motor car exports have claimed the most attention, and by early 1981 had resulted in a wave of protectionist moves by the US and European governments which were dressed up rather unconvincingly as a Japanese decision to exercise 'self-restraint'. Cars are Big Business, providing work for about 25 million people around the world in one way or another, and in European and American engineering industries that dependence is especially marked. In the Common Market countries there are 2 million jobs directly attached to the motor industry and a further 4 million around it. British Leyland alone is reckoned by some estimates to provide work for 1 million people in the UK, and in some other EEC countries the importance of motor manufacturing is, not suprisingly, greater still. West Germany has eighteen per cent of all industrial employment linked to the motor industry, against an EEC average of fourteen per cent. The industry is also crucial to the economic balance sheet of Europe, for up to twelve per cent of all industrial exports are automobiles, and, if those sales are related to the European Community's mounting oil import bill, they actually produce a twenty per cent trade surplus for the EEC.[16]

But Europe and the US have notoriously been losing out all the way to the Japanese. And although the problem became acute in 1980, it had been working away quietly for a full ten years before then. In 1970 the European motor manufacturers' share of the world export market for cars was 51 per cent, and that of the Japanese companies was only fifteen per cent. By 1980 the positions had been smartly reversed, with the European car producers hanging on to only 22 per cent while Japan had taken 45 per cent. The 'third markets', those open to the purest form of competition, had gone first, generally unnoticed by all but motor industry analysts, and by the late 1970s Japan was ready to turn on its European competitors' own home markets.

The Japanese industry had also inflicted heavy punishment on the US automobile industry in Detroit, and was at the same time pushing its European competitors in the American small cars market to one side with almost contemptuous ease. Recession and the Japanese invasion have cut Detroit's automobile industry employment from 1 million people in 1978 to 670,000 in 1981 with some experts suggesting that the workforce will be cut by almost 50 per cent more only in the three years to 1984 and nearly two-thirds by 1986.[17] Small wonder that a large and angry sign outside the United Automobile Workers' union headquarters on East Jefferson Avenue in Detroit reads: '300,000 laid-off UAW workers don't like your import. Please park it in Tokyo.' Visitors to Solidarity House are usually warned by UAW officials that on no account should they arrive in a foreign car, let alone a Japanese one.

The mood in Europe is now almost as sour, even if the Japanese at present have twice as large a share of the US market as they have of the European one. In 1980, Japan's motor manufacturers mounted a determined assault on the Common Market countries, pushing their sales up from 640,000 cars the year before to 785,000 as part of an overall campaign that saw their world exports rise 29 per cent during that year, when markets were really shrinking. In those EEC countries unprotected by the questionable devices employed by France and Italy to keep the Japanese out, the damage was serious. Japanese car sales to West Germany shot up by 43 per cent, giving Japan more than ten per cent of the market, and in the Benelux countries it grabbed a quarter of the market.

Retaliation against the Japanese was inevitable. But it is highly unlikely that the round of 'self-restraint' limits Japan accepted with European countries as well as the US in the summer of 1981 is by any means the end of the story. To begin with, in Japanese eyes, the Europeans still have a lot of fat to shed, while being very short of the productive industrial muscle they need to defend their markets.

Western Europe as a whole still occupies the top slot as the world's largest producer of motor vehicles. Japan is easily the biggest single producing country, with about 11 million units a year, but the EEC manufactures 10·5 million units and with other European countries such as Sweden and Spain the total reaches 12·4 million units. The US and the USSR-Comecon output bring up the rear with 8 million and 3 million units respectively. It may be unfair to lump all the European producers together, but the Japanese tend to regard them as an economic bloc, even though it suits their purposes to use divisive 'bi-lateral' tactics when actually negotiating with them.

In terms of productivity, and therefore output cost, Japan cannot help challenging all the European producers for what it sees as the supremacy of motor manufacturing. Each European car worker currently produces 12–15 cars a year, while his Japanese counterpart turns out 30–40 cars. The highly efficient new production line built by BL at Longbridge now produces 19–20 Mini Metros per man/year, and BL's senior management believes that eventually that rate can be improved to 24–25. But analysts suggest that by that time the Japanese average output per car worker will have increased to 50 cars per year. In other words, by the mid-1980s Japan's average car plant will still be twice as efficient as one of Europe's most advanced factories.[18]

Equally worrying is the dead set that Japanese industry appears to be making for the extremely lucrative car components sector. During the 1980s the components that go into a car, and which provide so much engineering employment, are likely to represent about 60 per cent of the vehicle's value with assembly accounting for the remaining 40 per cent. There are already signs that Japanese industry intends to wrest a major share of that business away from European and US suppliers, and the fact that ten per cent of a car's worth is expected to be in micro-electronic equipment reinforces that challenge.[19]

If the European motor manufacturers are unable to compete with Japan, and if their governments at the same time refuse to let die an industry that is central to their economies as well as of strategic importance for defence, what are the alternatives? Co-operation is one avenue. Japan's Nissan is showing the way with its proposed UK venture for producing up to 200,000 vehicles in Britain by 1986, its joint venture with Italy's state-owned Alfa-Romeo aiming at 60,000 units a year by 1983 and its deal with Motor-Iberica in Spain. But the 'if you can't beat them, join them' approach of European governments nevertheless risks being swamped by the many European producers who would rather opt for protection.

In 1981, the EEC motor manufacturers grouped in the Committee of Common Market Automobile Constructors (CCMC) produced a blueprint for protectionism. It proposed a single regime, to be imposed on the Japanese for five years by all Community countries, that would limit Japan's car sales as well as those of vehicles up to 3·5 tonnes. It took as its basis Japan's 1979 sales, arguing that the boost during 1980 had been a sort of pre-emptive strike aimed at improving the Japanese negotiating position. Thus the absolute maximum Japan would be allowed to sell in the EEC would be set at 579,000 cars and 56,000 light commercial vehicles, and attached to that was a set of further rigorous conditions. For 1982 the Japanese would not be permitted to gain more than twenty per cent of any individual Common Market country's market, and for the big producer nations such as Britain, France, West Germany and Italy that limit was set at six per cent. Furthermore, any attempts by the Japanese to circumvent these ceilings by local assembly would be added into the quotas unless those assemblies consisted of at least 80 per cent local content, to ensure that the Japanese producers did not use such plants as a funnel for Japanese components. As if to demonstrate how heady a tonic protectionism can be, the CCMC added that 'for the purposes of equity' the same conditions should be applied to Eastern European motor manufacturers.

In the meantime, while all this sabre rattling goes on, there is a school of thought that the European manufacturers have failed to identify their most dangerous enemy of the 1980s. The real enemy without will be the US, once its industry's gigantic 1980–85 investment drive is over and $75–80 billion have been sunk in highly automated new plant and equipment. Detroit's first target will be to re-capture its own home market with a new generation of 'downsized' fuel-efficient cars, which, as the Japanese currently have about 22 per cent of the US market, will intensify pressure on Europe. But Detroit's planned comeback also means that Europe will have an enemy within to contend with. Part of the new US strategy is to produce 'world cars' capable of grabbing export markets and helping pay off those massive investments. Many of the 'world cars' series will be produced inside Europe, with General Motors' plans to make 270,000 of them a year in Spain potentially just a pilot.

The elements of bitter transatlantic dissension are there, and, if the prize is a large stake in the shrinking but valuable automobile market, the recent rumblings of US-EEC trade wars over steel and petro-chemicals will doubtless pale into insignificance beside what lies in store. For the meantime, though, the Japanese are set to remain the object of both European and US resentment, even if many trade experts believe that Japan has in many ways been unfairly singled out as a whipping boy.

Japan's nuisance effect is that it concentrates on just a few acutely sensitive industrial sectors, rather than spreading its export drive more widely across a range of markets, in such a way as to earn the same amounts of foreign currency while being less identifiable and disruptive. As a proportion of its GNP, however, Japan's exports account for only ten per cent, while the US and Europe have a quarter of their economies made up by foreign trade. Japan is still only helping itself to a fairly modest slice of the world trade cake.

It is even possible to juggle the figures of Japan's soaring trade surpluses in a benign way that helps put them into perspective. Endymion Wilkinson, a British Eurocrat at the European Commission who for some years handled the EEC's economic relations in Tokyo, has calculated that on a per capita basis European-Japanese trade was until very recently in balance. In 1980 each Japanese represented $67 worth of imports from the EEC and each European $67 worth from Japan. He has also pointed out, intriguingly, that during the 1960s and up to the mid-1970s European and American failures to develop their export markets in Japan could owe something to the fact that they had so few businessmen based there that they were well outnumbered by the Christian missionaries being sent out. Judging by their successes, the missionaries could well have taught the representatives of industry a thing or two about hard-sell.[20]

The Japanese tend to be perplexed by allegations that they deliberately resist importing foreign goods other than the raw materials they require. They point to tariffs that, since they joined the GATT, the world's free traders 'club', in the mid-1950s as a 'developing' nation, have been reduced to close to zero. But they naturally recognize that in an economy that is 90 per cent home-based the giant Japanese trading houses and corporations have the markets and the distribution systems neatly tied-up. Non-tariff barrier dodges that discourage or bar imports do exist, too. In the port of Yokohama, according to motor car importers in Tokyo, there are just two qualified inspectors charged with vetting foreign cars on a more or less individual basis. VW of West Germany has so far spent millions of dollars in its bid to secure a 'type approval' deal from the Japanese authorities that would permit models such as the Golf to be imported in bulk without pernickety inspection bottlenecks. It is sometimes a wonder that foreign car manufacturers even sell 60,000 vehicles a year to Japan.

The Japanese, when it comes down to it, are inclined to be somewhat disingenuous when discussing why it is that they import so few industrial manufactured goods. In a self-deprecating way they even refer to the Japanese language as the greatest non-tariff barrier of them all. But the realists, like leading Japanese economist Masamichi Hanabusa, are aware that Japan's longer-term interests are not best served by an increasingly heavy trade surplus. In a study sponsored by the Royal Institute of International Affairs, London's Chatham House, he wrote: 'If Japan aspires to be a more harmonious economic actor on the international scene for the remainder of this century, it must rapidly increase imports in order to reduce the large current account surplus.' That was in 1978, and his countrymen have yet to heed his call.[21]

The cost to Japan in international retaliation could be heavy. In economic terms first, and eventually in political terms too. Back in 1977 the econometric analysis and research wing of one of Japan's largest and most influential newspapers, *Nihon Keizai Shimbun,* carried out a private study of the likely effects of an imports embargo on Japanese products by the Common Market. It found that, assuming domestic consumption and other export markets could not absorb the goods, Japan's industrial production would drop 1·2 per cent, with the precision machinery industry hit almost ten per cent. If there were to be a US embargo, the report added, overall production would be hit twice as hard. Nobuhiro Nomura, the report's author, urged the avoidance of export drives centred on specific regions 'as such behaviour would lead to world-wide protectionism moves'.

In fact that analysis rather understates the dangers to Japan of protectionist action, possibly because it used 1975 figures and export levels are now much higher. It also underplays the problem common to industrial countries that super-industrialized Japan Inc. is only about a quarter of the entire economy – the rich, bulbous upper part of a spinning top, which if it wobbles can make the top slow down and fall.

More recent studies in Japan have been rather more alarmist.

The Industrial Bank of Japan produced estimates in 1981 of how a major cutback on car exports would affect the Japanese motor industry. It calculated that a twenty per cent reduction in automobile sales to the US would cost 45,000 jobs and slice $3 billion off the GNP. At the Sumitomo Bank in Tokyo the ripple effect of an export cutback was reckoned to be greater than that. It reported that a ten per cent reduction on Japan's 1980 sales level to the US of 1·8 million vehicles would cost 47,000 jobs not just in the motor industry but also in steel and petro-chemicals. That, then, would be a consequence of losing 180,000 car exports a year for a country that is currently exporting over half a million cars a month to the world market. And those are core industrial jobs that support a multiplication of other jobs in sub-contracting industry and services. Japan's analysts are beginning to see that the reverse of the coin of concentrating on a handful of high technology, high profit sectors for its export drive is that those key industries are very vulnerable to retaliation.

If Japan does become the victim of protectionist barriers, there is of course one potentially huge and undeveloped sector that could rapidly mop-up a lot of Japanese industrial over-capacity: defence. It is also, understandably, one of the most ticklish and sensitive issues in Japan.

To say that Japan is still shocked into pacifism by the trauma of Hiroshima and Nagasaki is only partly true. Both internally and externally Japan has for some time been involved in a heated debate on defence, and the argument seems to be going the way of those who urge serious rearmament. The pressures from outside are perhaps the greatest, for as an economic super-power Japan is increasingly being urged to assume its responsibilities and ensure greater political stability by becoming the policeman of South East Asia.

The need for Japan to do so has certainly become more pressing since the end of the Vietnam War, for the US military presence in the North Pacific area has been reduced by seven-eighths and there are fears that a military vacuum has been created. US demands that Japan play a military role in the world are by no means new. In 1953, only a few short years after Japan had adopted its post-war constitution 'forever' renouncing 'the threat or use of force', the new reality of the Korean War had prompted the Americans to change their minds about Japanese militarism. At the Ikeda-Robertson conference that year, the US and Japanese governments agreed to promote militarism among the Japanese people to increase public support for Japan's re-armament.[22]

The strictly pacifist conditions of Article 9 of the Japanese constitution have long been abandoned. Japan re-interpreted its meaning to allow a self-defence force consisting of a highly conventional army and naval and air power of such limited range that in practical terms it has no offensive capability. But defence spending that still totals less than $10 billion a year, or one per cent of GNP, is widely considered inadequate by Japan's allies, who point out that as things stand they have to assure the protection even of Japan's oil supply routes. At MIT, Lester Thurow makes the point that if the US is to 'handicap' itself with President Reagan's military re-equipment programme, not only Europe but also Japan will be pushed to do much the same 'never mind the political consequences'.

Japan's inching toward renewed militarism is described by one analyst as a 'Kabuki-like epic', reminiscent of the country's intricate and unhurried sixteenth-century school of drama in which plots unfold at a snail's pace.[23] But there are internal pressures that could accelerate events, and which are possibly more insistent than US demands or even neighbouring China's recent appeal that Japan should double its defence costs.

Leading companies such as Mitsubishi are believed to have suggested that a powerful fillip would be given to Japanese industry if it were to re-enter the international arms business. According to some observers in Tokyo, the industrial lobby's murmurings of dissatisfaction at being denied the research and development flywheel of defence have of late been swelling to a chorus of protest. Japan's tiny aviation industry, which is about a thirtieth of the size of its US counterpart, would be among the first to benefit, as would shipbuilding where sluggish world demand has also seriously damped growth.

Whether the genuine spirit of pacifism that exists in much of Japanese society will withstand these various pressures it is impossible to tell. What is certain is that Japan's peaceful conquest of the markets of South East Asia has now given it the leadership of the 'co-prosperity sphere' that it sought through war. But perhaps one should recall that in the Japan of the 1920s there was also a pacifist movement, and a decade later the country was preparing to enforce co-prosperity on its neighbours through military means.

The key to future developments in Japan is naturally held by the US. If the Reagan administration gives in to further demands for protection against Japanese industry, events could move swiftly. The enduring example of America's capacity to disrupt economic balance in the world is the 1930 Smoot-Hawley tariff, when in the shock of the Great Depression protectionists pushed through legislation that erected the highest tariff walls around the US market since the industrial revolution. The effect was shattering. Closure of the American export market to European producers soon provoked a tide of bankruptcies and defaults on the largely US loans that had funded much of Europe's post-World War I reconstruction. Before long the international community had split into rival trading and currency blocs, whose weapons in the new trade wars were competitive currency devaluations and aggressively price-cutting export drives.

The impact on employment was dramatic. Far from saving jobs, the US action during 1931 pushed the total number of jobless from 4 million to 10 million, and by 1933 16 million Americans were out of work. In all, the advanced industrial countries saw their combined unemployment rise from about 5 million in 1929 to almost 25 million in 1932. Six million of them were in Germany alone, and, well in advance of Nazism, Franco-German relations were severely strained by radical deflationary policies in Germany that cut export prices and elbowed France out of its crucial East European markets.

The protectionists' hand is once again being strengthened by the slow-down in the US economy, which during the 1970s is calculated by the New York Stock Exchange to have grown at only 65 per cent of the rate attained during the 1960s.[24] American analysts now suggest that President Reagan's cabinet is more or less evenly divided on the issue of tariff protection, in itself a reflection of the conflict of interests now splitting US industry and banking. While domestic US industries such as steel and textiles are lending their weight to the demands for import controls of the automobile manufacturers and some electronics producers, ranged against them is the might of American multi-national corporations and the major banks. Wall Street is understandably worried that any protectionist moves would stifle first of all the exports of Third World industries and so de-stabilize that precarious structure of LDC debt. The multi-nationals have a similar vested interest in uninhibited world trade, for many of them have up to half of their assets locked into countries that would be among the first victims of US protectionism. One US expert has emphasized that the power of these companies with a vital interest in free trade should not be underestimated, and cites the 65 corporations grouped in the 'Emergency Committee for American Trade', a lobbying organization formed in 1967 which includes Bank of America, Chase, Citibank, Cargill, Exxon, Honeywell, IBM, Sperry Rand, Texas Instruments, TRW and Xerox and represents annual worldwide sales of $500 billion.[25]

He describes their muscle as an inexorable force that has now met the immovable object of America's traditional industries in the domestic market. With US unemployment liable on a number of estimates to reach ten per cent before very long, he adds: 'Politically, the clamour for protectionism will be insistent and impossible to ignore.' A political quirk that appears to strengthen the protectionists' grasp of the initiative in this struggle is that support for trade barriers now crosses traditional party alignments in the US. The Republicans are historically the party of traditional Northern industry, while the Democrats owe much of their backing to the trade unions that are now the shrillest in their calls for protection.

In Europe, the strains of protectionism are if anything more pronounced and the persistent worry on both sides of the Atlantic is that trade restrictions by one or all of the Common Market countries could trigger massive US retaliation. Arthur Dunkel, director general of the GATT (General Agreement on Tariffs and Trade) has described this consideration as acting so far as 'a kind of balance of terror' that has staved-off trade war. But the omens for that state of affairs continuing are not good. Bill Brock, who is President Reagan's special trade representative and a US cabinet member, warned in Brussels in mid-1981 that Washington was prepared to wage 'an export credits war' if the EEC failed to cut the interest rate subsidies being paid by European governments to boost agricultural exports.[26]

Export credit rates that permit companies to under-cut competitors are a continuing source of friction between the US and Europe, while the whole question of government subsidies has also become a divisive issue setting most of the European countries at each other's throats. Cash bail-outs to industrial lame ducks have developed into a vicious and costly game of 'beggar-my-neighbour' inside the Common Market that now threatens to undermine some of its firmest foundations.

West Germany's Chancellor Helmut Schmidt shocked other EEC heads of government in early 1981 when he warned that he was prepared to ignore the Common Market in steel, which was in fact the fore-runner of the present day Community, and impose border levies on steel produced by other EEC countries that had been subsidizing that industry. Schmidt said that he was not prepared 'to see one more Dortmund steelworker lose his job' because of unfair subsidies. Although West Germany is generally a staunch defender of free trade, with that phrase the Chancellor joined the ranks of Mrs Thatcher and President Reagan, who also speak of fair trade when threatening protectionist measures.

The detailed four-part study of EEC protectionism carried out by European Research Associates, mentioned earlier in this chapter, predicts that as a result of its internal conflicts the EEC faces a future of 'Balkanisation'. The authors assume 'rising unemployment levels approaching or perhaps surpassing twenty per cent of the industrial workforce in the 1980s', and foresee the unity of the Common Market being eroded to a 'patchwork of essentially protectionist states involved in increasingly bitter quarrels'.

The rot could be said to have set in with the sharp increase during the early 1970s of what is now being called 'financial protectionism', meaning subsidies intended to save jobs at the likely expense of those in the same industry elsewhere in Europe. Britain's entry into the EEC in 1973 to some extent rolled back that tide for a while, because it brought with it an EEC-EFTA tariff dismantlement turning Western Europe into a huge free trade area that set an example to the world. Today 65 per cent of the EEC countries' export business is with other European nations, and, while the Community's tariff-free character has not been changed, the use of non-tariff barriers by various European governments is creating growing alarm.

Italy is increasingly pointed to as one of the chief culprits, yet all EEC states seem guilty to some degree. France and Italy have for several years been quarrelling over trade in knitted clothing, and it has been France that generally resorts to underhand tactics to block shipments from the Italians. Early in 1981, though, Italy gave the rest of Europe a master class lesson in how to create non-tariff barriers on a breathtaking scale. To prevent unwanted steel from entering the country, it suddenly withdrew its customs officers on a bureaucratic pretext from more than half of the 23 designated entry points along the frontiers. Almost the first victim of this manoeuvre was a West German ship loaded with steel products, which was forced to lie idle in the Italian port of Piombino while Bonn and a number of other governments made urgent and angry representations to Rome. The UK motor industry is also not convinced that all its European partners play fair, so Britain's Society of Motor Manufacturers and Traders has opened an enquiry into the devices it suspects France and Germany of employing to cut down UK car exports. As demand in Europe shrinks, overcapacity in major industries grows and massive redundancies loom, the list of tit-for-tat protectionist squabbles grows.

West Germany's reaction to such developments is widely seen to be crucial. Some observers support the Bonn government's contention that ending the subsidies race in steel, shipbuilding and engineering is the only way to guarantee the survival of free trade and the EEC. Others are frankly suspicious of German motives, and believe that it amounts to a German gambit to force to the wall less productive competitors and industries, now at a delicate transitional stage as they attempt to restructure. It would be survival of the fittest, not the neediest, and thus a contradiction of the Community's role of promoting co-operation and economic convergence. The Brussels consultants who analysed protectionism go a step further and suggest that Germany's notion of free trade – which they say has been 'an essentially mercantilist policy based on an undervalued exchange rate and the amassing of huge trade surpluses' – will destroy EEC trade and therefore Germany's own exports.

West Germany at least defends the spirit of free trade. The greater risk to the system is likely to come from those countries where influential economists are calculating the short term gain in jobs saved that could be yielded by resorting to import controls. Britain, with its resentful offshore approach to continental Europe and growing susceptibility to 'siege economy' measures, is the most outstanding example. Since 1975, the Cambridge Economic Policy Group has been arguing the case for selective import controls, and, once unemployment began to rise sharply the siren song of trade barriers to halt import penetration has become increasingly attractive politically. The Cambridge Group is sometimes viewed as the unruly maverick of economic theorists, brilliant but wrong-headed, but its job-saving promises not long ago received a semi-official boost. Using the Treasury's econometric model computer, analysts reporting

to Westminster MPs found it was 'possible to design an import
control simulation that will have very beneficial results on unemployment'. In June 1979 they carried out an exercise with the
Treasury computer, in which an assumption that just over half of
the UK's imports of manufactured goods were 'stabilized' at
1978 levels, coupled with some tax cuts, yielded a drop in unemployment of 630,000 people by 1983. The report added that the
job saving effects would almost certainly become progressive as
time went on.[27]

Some of the more respectable options being offered as an
alternative to creeping or even deliberate protectionism are,
unfortunately, just as perilous. One blueprint for European
recovery recognizes that Europe's wage rates are instrumental
in pricing its industries out of world markets, combined with low
productivity that has often resulted from attempts to limit unemployment, and suggests as an answer a deliberate and concerted
effort to drop wages closer to average international rates of pay.
If, as seems inevitable, that were politically impossible, it rec-
ommends currency devaluation.

Jostling for advantage through currency adjustment smacks of
the 1930s, for it would probably spark a round of competitive
devaluations by other industrialized countries. The net result of
any devaluations, on a scale big enough to counter high manufacturing costs, would furthermore be an enormous jump in countries' oil import bills and the likelihood of rampant hyper-inflation. More to the point, perhaps, the Europeans and the US may
feel they need increased export business to get their economies
moving again, but they really have no right to it. Their hold on
the world's trade in manufactured goods may have been slipping
since the end of World War II, but they still have over two-thirds
of the total. According to some figures, the combined manufactured exports of Japan, the newly-industrialized countries, such
as Brazil, South Korea etc, the less developed countries of the
Third World and the Comecon state-trading countries of Eastern
Europe, including the USSR, amount to just 30 per cent of the
world market.[28]

Slow growth in the size of that market is the basic problem. Industrial production, geared to serve the boom conditions that lasted over a quarter of a century, now outstrips demand. World trade grew only one per cent in 1980–1,[29] as against averages of up to ten per cent annually before that. It used to be said that the credit system provided by the international monetary structure provided 'the oil that lubricates the machinery of international trade'. In retrospect it was, of course, oil itself, or rather cheap oil, that was the real lubricant.

Creating new demand that will keep the rich North Atlantic countries in work and wealth is becoming an urgent necessity. The best way would be the hard way; re-cycling the OPEC petrodollar surpluses, but still virtually giving away jobs and goods to the poor South to prime those huge markets and eventually restore momentum to the world's economies. The more tempting and easy way is the way of the late 1930s, with all that that implies.

The world's military spending bill is currently being put at an astounding $450 billion a year.[30] The moral, let alone political, implications of that are clear enough to most people. The Brandt Report pointed out that all official development aid for the Third World totals less than five per cent of that arms bill, while a mere 0·05 per cent of that sum could, if spent on agricultural development, make the poor countries of the world self-sufficient in food production within ten years.

But armaments production is potentially an attractive option to many Western governments. Its benefits in net jobs are disproportionately low in relation to the capital sums involved, but its high technology character has considerable generative powers that would help downstream industries. American experience of the prosperity that accompanied the Vietnam War years inevitably increases the attractions of producing arms, and for Europeans there is the comparatively recent example of the arms race that began in the mid-1930s.

Rearmament in pre-war Britain had the effect in the two years up to 1937 of re-launching the battered engineering industries and producing a subsequent boom in consumer industries. Peter Ludlow, a leading economic historian, reckons that at the outbreak of war the UK was in fact on a more developed war footing than Germany, where the arms build-up had had similarly beneficial effects on the economy. From mass unemployment of 6 million in Germany in the early part of the decade there had, by 1937, been such a turnaround that Italian and Yugoslav guest workers were being brought in to ease the labour shortage. Ludlow goes so far as to describe Hitler's war as a means of securing even more labour without the inconvenience of having to wait for, say, Polish and Czech guest workers to come to Germany. For the German working man the benefits of rearmament were considerable. As Hilter contemplated the invasion of Britain in 1940, German workers were holidaying on the beaches of Northern Europe in record numbers and free collective bargaining had just been introduced.

Defence spending is often said to be the only form of demand management, stimulation of the economy, that conservative governments consider respectable. The Reagan administration's planned boost to arms production while slashing almost all other public spending is a prime example. Yet the notion that Western governments will be increasingly seduced into spending a Soviet Union-style 11–13 per cent of GNP on military hardware and defence still begs a single question.

Who is going to fight whom? And why, or for what, would they fight? There are, amongst the major economies, no clearcut enemies that the Western industrialized powers can identify as dyed-in-the-wool political villains comparable to the fascist states of 45 years ago or the worldwide 'conspiracy' of the Communist International. An objective analyst would probably conclude from a look at the post-war nuclear age that Moscow's behaviour has been overall as cautious and responsible as that of Washington and the other NATO powers, and that only a threat by the Warsaw Pact against the Middle East oilfields would represent a genuine *casus belli*.

At the same time, most people would consider it inconceivable that, even without the buffer of the Common Market in its present form, France and Germany would ever again go to war. It seems still less likely that the Europeans as a whole would find their interests so opposite to those of North America that some sort of transatlantic conflict could ensue. While Japan might represent a more probable enemy, not least because of the underlying racialism of both sides and the still raw memories of World War II, the Japanese are at present not heavily enough armed to be a viable foe.

All these are reassuring points. There are others less so, and beyond them lies the spectre of an economic collapse as swift and widespread as that of the early 1930s. If that decade has any lesson to teach, it is that in the flux following a breakdown in international co-operation a new and volatile breed of politics is quickly born. The 30 wars at present being fought around the world – often called the 'proxy' wars that help provide a safety valve for the rivalries of the super-powers – would almost all provide a short fuse in a world grown tense.

8

Make-work Schemes – Miracles or Mirage?

Silly statistics have a charm all of their own. If all the people in the world were to stand shoulder to shoulder, they could fit on to the Isle of Wight. If the world were the size of a billiard ball, it would be a billion times smoother. And, if all the girls attending the Harvard Ball were laid from end to end, Dorothy Parker wouldn't have been at all surprised.

Here's a new one. If the real costs of unemployment in the industrial countries for just a single year were grossed up in dollar bills, those banknotes would carpet not just Europe but the whole of Africa as well.[1]

In crude terms the price of 25 million jobless during 1981 in the 24 OECD countries amounted to a breathtaking five hundred billion dollars – $500,000,000,000. It is not a figure that would find favour with some purists, because it combines money cost with money lost, but it is at least arrived at by adding oranges and tangerines, not apples and oranges. Figuring out the scale of unemployment's financial burden is complicated, risky and the subject of endless academic argument, but it is also essential to combating the crisis.

Unemployment costs everyone money, unemployed and employed alike, for the cost is not just in the 'dole drain' of benefits and in reduced tax receipts that have to be made up by those still at work. It must also be measured in lost production, which has the effect of shrinking the economy and cutting everybody's standard of living.

Assessing just how expensive the jobs crisis has been and will become is important because many governments still believe that they cannot 'afford' to spend more on measures that might put people back to work. Once it is acknowledged how much money is really gurgling away down the drain in terms of cash cost and wealth lost, decisions to promote and create work become more likely. Instead of wasting the money, the political emphasis will shift to investing it in work.

First, though, it would be sensible to make a distinction between making work and creating work. The two sound alike yet they are really very different. In a way they are even total opposites. The former is the art of finding work for more people, and also of reducing the number of people who are in the market to do that work. Re-dividing work could eventually go a substantial way towards helping solve the jobs problem, but it still comes down to cutting much the same sized cake into smaller pieces.

Work creation, on the other hand, involves the baking of a bigger cake. It is the expansion of the number of jobs available in order to meet the demand for work, as opposed to a re-distribution of the same number of jobs. Sometimes the line between the two can blur a little, in spite of that fundamental difference, but so far as possible the creation of new jobs has been deliberately separated off into the following chapter.

That might suggest that this chapter concerns merely the division of old work, the same over-manning and rejection of productivity improvements that have brought most of the industrialized nations to their present plight. At first sight the idea of sharing out what work there is – the new heresy of 'work-sharing' now being professed by Europe's trade unions – looks absurd. On closer examination, however, a re-jigging of 'working time', beginning with education and training and running right through to early retirement, not only has a good deal to recommend it but also seems increasingly inevitable if social and political chaos is to be avoided.

The trick will be to avoid saddling industry with the sort of mounting costs and sinking profits that have over the past twenty years led to its being able to employ fewer people because manufacturing was itself shrinking.

That difficult feat is made no easier by the further need to avoid simply shuffling people across on to government payrolls except in carefully considered circumstances.

The speed and determination with which working time adjustments are made would be greatly influenced if the size of the sums that joblessness is already costing became common political currency. It might then become clear that finance ministries' grudging reluctance to find funds for manpower programmes is short-sighted and risks being dangerously counterproductive.

So how expensive are the dole queues? In February 1981 British Treasury officials provoked 'oohs' and 'aahs' in the House of Commons with an article in the government's Economic Progress Report putting the cost of each increase in UK unemployment of 100,000 at £340 million. What they did not add was that there are good grounds for believing that the true cost to the British economy is actually four times that figure – over £1·25 billion for every 100,000 unemployed.

In the careful manner of Whitehall mandarins, the Treasury experts told the precise truth. The fiscal cost to the British exchequer, meaning the outgoings in benefits taken together with lost revenues and even adjusted with higher administrative costs, totalled £340 million. So the misleading impression that gives is *suggestio falsi* rather than *suppressio veri*. The article did indeed stress its concern with direct costs only, but somewhat confused the issue by saying that, if unemployment rose because of a decline in economic activity, then corporation tax receipts would drop, although, if instead it was caused by policies aimed at making industry more efficient, then those receipts might rise.

It is not, of course, in Treasury ministers' interest to encourage speculation on what the true cost of unemployment might be, because their role is to oppose attempts to 'spend our way out of trouble'. Therefore the temptation is to play down the seriousness of the trouble, which is no doubt why Leon Brittan,

Chief Secretary to the Treasury, gave short shrift to any back-bencher in Parliament who attempted to make sense of those Treasury figures.

Grossing up the Treasury calculations can be misleading, as the Chief Secretary told the House of Commons when an MP on the Opposition benches attempted to multiply the total of registered unemployed by £3400 to get £8·5 billion. The reason is that the mixture of ages, sex and former occupation of the 100,000 people analysed for the Treasury's calculation is almost certainly changing the whole time. But if that Treasury figure is not a useful basis for estimating the direct fiscal costs to the Exchequer of the joblessness totals, what was the object of the exercise in the first place?

As the wrangling goes on it becomes still more confusing. Leon Brittan later conceded in the House of Commons that the average fiscal cost of each registered unemployed person was probably 'nearer', meaning apparently over, £3500, which suggests that the sample chosen for the Treasury calculation may even have been a rather cheaper mix of age, sex and former job.[2] In the House of Lords, meanwhile, fresh estimates put the fiscal cost of a jobless married man with two children at just over £6000 a year, and that of a single man on the same previous average wage at £5236 a year. Parallel to all this confusion there are other lines of argument. There is the view that serious long term unemployment eventually works out cheaper, because thanks largely to the front-end loading of redundancy payments to some workers and of supplementary benefits to others the State's outlay eventually decreases. Thus in the first year of unemployment a miner might cost £6810 and in the second £5732.[3] Then, almost contrariwise, there is the argument that while a private sector worker who becomes unemployed certainly costs the Exchequer, someone who was formerly employed in the public sector may even be saving the state money by joining the dole queue. That comes into the same 'every cloud has a silver lining' category as the reminder by one government minister not long ago that, 'To the extent that a rise in unemployment is due to an excessive level of wage settlements, the tax the government recoups on those excessive settlements is greater than the amount of tax it loses as a result of the consequent unemployment.'[4]

By the end of 1981, the government's own Manpower Services Commission had chimed in with figures that were not only higher than those of the Treasury, but also apparently sounder. The MSC put the cost to the Exchequer of each person on the dole at £4380, and was not bashful about multiplying that average cost by the number of registered unemployed. For the whole of 1981 it assumed an average figure of 2·84 million, and so arrived at a total direct cost of £12·45 billion. The reason that the MSC's per capita figure was over £1000 a year greater was, it turned out, that it was including what is known as the 'second round' effects on the government's indirect tax revenues. Because the unemployed can spend less than people in work, their reduced contributions of Value Added Tax can also be added to the calculation.

If Britain is having difficulty deciding on the direct and calculable expense of unemployment, it is not surprising that the hidden effects – sometimes known as the 'opportunity costs' – have scarcely figured in the debate. But in West Germany an analysis of the overall financial burden has been carried out, and it suggests convincingly that the invisible costs of lost production are considerably higher than the fiscal loss. As a rule-of-thumb, some experts had been suggesting that the reductions in output, that are both the cause and effect of unemployment, would be roughly equal to the direct fiscal loss. So that, in very rough terms, one could multiply the Exchequer cost by two to get the real cost. A group of German economists at the IAB Federal Employment Institute in Nuremberg have indicated that it would be closer to the mark to multiply by four.[5]

Looking at the situation in West Germany in 1978, when there were 1·3 million unemployed, they produced the following calculations. The fiscal cost of the half million people who qualified for unemployment benefit at that time was around 12 billion

Deutschemarks, and the further three-quarter of a million jobless receiving different types of benefit were reckoned to cost another DM 11·3 billion. The direct cost therefore amounted to a little over DM 23 billion. The losses attributable to loss of production through insufficient employment that year were put, following a set of complicated calculations, at DM 74 billion. That figure, which was equivalent to a stunning 5·5 per cent of West Germany's GNP in 1978, was based on a set of assumptions that the Nuremberg economists claimed were very conservative. The factors they based their figures on – such as losses of income and the slowdown in consumption – were deliberately handicapped in order to produce a lower final figure. The authors prefaced their findings with the comment that, if they had based their assumptions on more buoyant times and if over 1 million foreign guest workers had not returned home and if there were no restraints on productivity improvements in German industry, the bottom line would have been DM 127 billion.

The German study's findings on the invisible costs are not very different to a similar analysis attempted by the European Trades Union Institute in Brussels. Taking 1979 figures, researchers there assessed that the average potential productivity of each worker in the EEC was around $18,500 a year.[6] With Community unemployment that year at six million people rather than the structural 2 million that had earlier been the norm, they put lost output at $75 billion, or 4·5 per cent of the EEC's gross domestic product.

By their very nature, these opportunity costs are extremely vulnerable to criticism and even outright dismissal by the purists. They are an arithmetical calculation of loss and not cost. It is easy enough for those who wish to reject them to insist that political and economic management is concerned with the situation as it is rather than what it might have been. That naturally begs the question that it is also about what it could be.

Even more liable to criticism are any attempts to transfer such opportunity cost calculations from one country to another. The Nuremberg economists' calculation of the direct fiscal cost of 1·3 million registered unemployed was interestingly close to the £4·5 billion figure that grossing up the Treasury's figures would give for 1·3 million jobless in the UK. But there would no doubt be howls of protest from the Treasury experts, were any politician to try applying the opportunity cost 'times 4 formula' to the likely fiscal burden of 3 million unemployed in Britain and to arrive at a grand total of £40 billion a year.

Adding 2 + 2 and risking the answer 5 *is* dangerous, and no one would seriously advocate basing economic policies on conjecture. Yet to ignore the probable opportunity cost and reject it as a major economic consideration would seem to defy common sense. It is such huge 'ball park' estimates as a total financial cost of $500 billion to the OECD countries in 1981 alone that make the idea of working time adjustments an attractive first line of defence in most of those countries' war on unemployment.

Work-sharing has obvious social and political advantages, but it also has more to recommend it in economic terms than its anti-productivity nature at first suggests. If more people are working and earning a living, they can afford to consume more, so the market for goods and services expands. There are some dangerous snags, notably that all those extra workers also boost the price of the goods being produced and cheaper imports could be sucked into Britain's expanded markets. Hence some economists' insistence that protectionist import controls should be used to cocoon the UK economy.

It is vital to break out of the present trap of rising direct and indirect unemployment costs and sinking consumption and demand. Putting people back to work in any way available could have much the same effect as cranking an old wind-up gramophone just as it is slowing to a cacophonous growl. Some of the projections made by the advocates of work-sharing claim that it would be a short cut to almost full employment. The term 'work-sharing' now covers a good deal more than the reduction of the working week, so that more employees would be taken on by a company to produce the same quantity of goods. It spans early retirement, extra training, education, longer holidays, sabbatical leaves, with a shorter working week and reductions of 'systematic' overtime now the central elements. West German experts have calculated that a judicious mixture, relying more on the fringe elements than the much more controversial central ones, could by themselves yield dramatic results. They reckon they could take over 1 million people off the payrolls of German companies – and so allow that number to move off the dole queues on to the payrolls – by extending schooling and apprenticeship training for a year, lowering retirement ages by a year, knocking just one hour off the working week and granting an extra day's holiday a year while also giving one employee in ten a fortnight a year of special educational leave.[7]

The same report also points out that, in theory, the suppression of overtime working in Germany, where it is not as prevalent as in Britain, would create 1·3 million new jobs. Estimates elsewhere of the effect of major cutbacks in working hours promise similar new employment opportunities. Just how great these are depends on the increases of productivity built into the calculation. As part of their campaign to sell work-sharing the trades unions of Europe have in effect been promising that, although companies would have more employees, they would at least be harder working employees.

The work-sharing formula that now establishes the basis of the unions case was set out in a document published in early 1980 by the European Trade Union Institute. Drawing on studies made in France, Germany, Belgium, Holland, Italy and the UK, it suggested that a ten per cent reduction in the working week, say from 40 hours to 36 hours, would in fact only push wage costs up by 5·5 per cent because of productivity gains. The unions' blandishment is that by working fewer hours employees would be able to accelerate their 'average daily work rhythm', and that absenteeism would also be cut. Without that compensating productivity rise, the whole concept becomes absurdly expensive, and in Britain the Federation of Mechanical Engineering Employers has claimed that the adoption of a 35-hour week would see labour costs rising by anywhere between fourteen and twenty per cent.

Just how much new work is made available depends arithmetically on how great the drop in working hours would be. The UK's Department of Employment has worked out that a 35-hour week, representing a 12·5 per cent contraction of the present week, could yield up to half a million new jobs. The Trade Union Research Unit, not surprisingly, has put that figure rather higher, at a maximum of 890,000. The productivity improvements are also crucial, and, if they were fairly negligible, those two estimates revise the effects of a 35-hour week in Britain down to 100,000 and 190,000 new jobs respectively. Guaranteed productivity breakthroughs are clearly in the unions' interest if they are to sell work-sharing as a source of jobs.

Just how successful they will be is still far from clear. In Brussels the European Commission is now putting its weight behind the move towards adjustments of working time in the wider sense, while some of its officials think that the pressures of joblessness in the EEC make work-sharing inevitable. The biggest push towards a 35-hour week, rather than the 42 hours currently worked in most European countries, has come with the election of Francois Mitterand to the French Presidency. In mid-1981, only days after his victory at the polls, his government set 1985 as the deadline by which the 35-hour week should be introduced, even though France's 'Patronat' employers' organization still opposes it, as do its counterparts elsewhere. In political terms, though, the British government appears to be alone in the EEC in being adamantly opposed to the idea.

The most probable outcome will be a gradual shift towards shorter hours, for that reduces the level of political controversy surrounding the issue and helps smooth out the cost. Trade union economists say that achieving a 35-hour week over two or three years would entail annual increases in wage and capital costs of only 2·2 per cent.[8] At the same time the unions in some countries are in any case prevented under the terms of wage bargains already struck from pressing the matter immediately; in West

Germany it has been placed on the back-burner until 1982–3 and in Italy it is thought unlikely to land on negotiating tables until 1983. In France, government officials think there is a natural drift towards a shorter week, so that on present trends, even without political pressure, French workers will by 1985 be on a 38½-hour week.

The key question in all this seems to be not so much the number of hours that people will be working by the mid-1980s, which risks being a red herring, but the number of people who will be working those hours. For work-sharing could have the reverse effect to that intended by its advocates. Employers could have their workers doing fewer hours more productively while refusing to take on extra labour.

A survey of European employers found that almost two-thirds would do just that. Only 30 per cent would take up the slack by employing more people, while the rest were inclined to fall back on rationalization and, if necessary, more overtime. The latter is, of course, the very opposite of work-sharing. Such attitudes are scarcely surprising in a world where companies have consistently been criticized for low productivity and poor profitability; where the cost of machinery is, thanks to micro-electronics, falling fast; and where the real costs of employing a single extra person are, thanks to all the fringe costs, considerably greater than getting ten existing employees to each produce just ten per cent more.[9]

The employers' strong temptation may well be to accept the drift towards shorter working hours, but to take the money and run. That can perhaps be dampened by various government incentives, so that the taxpayer foots the bill instead, but the facts of life are that high unemployment and a slack labour market tend to give employers the whip hand. Only highly skilled employees and people with specialist knowledge retain their bargaining power in a really poor labour market, and, as they are not the victims of the jobs crisis, they have no interest in pressing for work-sharing in any form.

That in turn casts a long shadow over hopes of tackling the problem of overtime. For although employers and trade unionists are allied in their public commitments to stamp out overtime working, both have formidable vested interests in retaining it. In Britain, which operates the highest overtime levels in Europe, a quarter of all manual workers put in about eight hours of overtime every week. Their interest in retaining the practice is clear enough, while for their employers the system provides not only the flexibility needed to cope with production crises but also value for money that is hard to argue against. Lest it seem that Britain's industrial record scarcely justifies systematic overtime, it might be worth pointing out that close behind the UK in the overtime stakes comes West Germany.[10]

Overtime is a can of worms. Both sides love it and loathe it, and each manages ingeniously to use it as a focus of mistrust. The unions say it is an employers' device to hide low levels of pay. The employers say it is a weapon of blackmail and industrial sabotage used by the workers to earn more than is their due. Trade unionists retort that overtime is a reflection of bad labour organization on the employers' part, and, although it is inefficient because productivity is poorer at the end of the working day, it is nevertheless a system that employers perpetuate by their refusal to create new jobs.[11] What is certain, to cut through all this mutual recrimination, is that excessive overtime eventually benefits neither the shopfloor nor the management. As John Morley, a key official in the European Commission's Social Affairs directorate, points out, overtime is 'now just a very bad habit' which in European industry can create a vicious circle. If an employer fails to keep his manufacturing plant up-to-date, he soon requires longer hours from his workforce to compensate for that inefficiency, while the increased wages and the poorer productivity that result from the overtime make it ever harder for him to make enough profits to catch up through installing modern machinery.

It is quite possible to operate industries without much more than a bare minimum of overtime to allow production flexibility. In Holland, Belgium and Denmark only about two per cent of all work is overtime, while in Germany and the UK the percentage has been estimated at six per cent and 7·5 per cent respectively.[12] Even more clearcut are the beneficial effects on employment that major overtime bans would have. In 1978, when in pre-recession Britain overtime was at a peak of about 16 million hours a week, the Department of Employment suggested that the elimination of overtime would alone be enough to eliminate all unemployment in manufacturing industry.[13] On a much more modest scale, if half of all the extra hours worked on top of a 48-hour week were banned, in other words just the tip of the overtime iceberg, that alone would create 100,000 new jobs in Britain.

Criticism of overtime, which is after all a system where a minority of workers are able to hog more work and money for themselves at the expense of others, is bound to increase as the jobs crisis deepens. But, as the old joke has it: 'When all is said and done, there is a great deal more said than done.' All the figures setting out the advantages of work-sharing seem very compelling, but fail to take one important point into consideration. In many industrial regions throughout Europe, well-qualified skilled workers are even now in short supply. There is no attraction for any employer to cut down on the use he can make of a skilled operative, if he cannot find others to take up the slack. Blanket statistics such as those advocating work-sharing tend to smother that sort of inconvenient reality.

None of this necessarily means that the self interest of a minority of the workforce will be able indefinitely to withstand the overwhelming need of industrial countries for work to be more widely distributed. What it does imply is that governments will have to bribe employers to take on more people. Even when the money is available, it is far from easy to design systems in which the government requirement of more jobs matches neatly with employers' wants. Throwing money at industry is by no means always successful. Sometimes it is expensive but produces minimal results, and there have been examples of it producing no lasting results at all.

In May 1979, the West Germans launched a massive job subsidies scheme which, when it had run its course over a year, had cost the taxpayers almost DM 1 billion. It was the Federal Republic's first sally into interfering with market forces through a manpower policy instrument of such size, and one German observer was even moved to declare: 'Later in history, this would be called the German version of supply-side economics.' If so, it might be cold comfort for President Reagan and his supply-siders, for in a number of ways it was a conspicuous failure. On the other hand, it provided information on the limitations of such schemes that could prove extremely valuable during the 1980s.

It demonstrated that some types of unemployment are very hard to eliminate, at any price, by artificial means. The West German programme addressed itself to a number of different employment problems, such as re-integrating the unskilled and long term unemployed back into work and training up people in industries where technological change was threatening to suppress jobs. It also concentrated on areas which at that time were unemployment blackspots with over six per cent joblessness. The subsidies on offer seemed compelling enough, consisting of up to 90 per cent wage cost subsidies for people undergoing retraining, 80 per cent for on-the-job training, and carrots to employers of 70–90 per cent subsidies covering the cost of taking on additional workers with no skills or who had been unemployed for a long time. The other important characteristic of the scheme was that it was run on what was called the 'greyhound principle', it was first come, first served for both employers and job hunters until the money ran out.

One of the first findings to emerge was that the greyhound system turned out to be 'about the worst policy design for creating lasting employment'.[14] This is partly because large subsidies are no substitute for carefully planned jobs that guarantee to pay for themselves once the subsidy runs out. Largely, though, it is because the unskilled and the long term unemployed, who are to a very great extent one and the same, are actually resistant to training of the sort that would integrate them into soundly-based jobs. On-the-job training under the German scheme was found to be a rewarding way of spending government money, but chiefly for workers who already had a skill. Low wage earners, paradoxically, are much less prone to opt for training that might make them higher earners unless they already have the guarantee of a job to go to afterwards.

Employers feel much the same way. They have profound misgivings about taking on labour, whatever the accompanying subsidy incentives, unless the new employee has skills that make it a profitable deal for the company.

If employers are wary of taking on hardcore unemployed, whatever the level of cash payments from government that should in theory make it a financially painless yet socially responsible arrangement, existing employees in the company can be downright hostile. Researchers checking on the effects of the West German scheme found that the taking on of a 'low performer' encountered resistance on the shopfloor because it was feared that overall output would therefore drop, and earnings with it.

That sounds logical enough, even if it is the exact opposite of what governments fear is the true economic effect of wage subsidies. For it is the danger that these subsidies in the first place endanger the survival of unsubsidized competitors, and in the second place push all wages up at an inflationary rate, that leads them to be seen as a double-edged sword. British experience during the second half of the 1970s, when many schemes now defunct were launched, has created a strong suspicion in Whitehall that special employment programmes may well fail to create many long term jobs, and instead create inflation. Ian Byatt, a senior Treasury official, observes, 'I suspect our regional employment subsidies "leaked" into wages. Analysis suggests that wages in special development areas tended to be higher than in the country as a whole.' In the UK's textiles and clothing industry, where the Temporary Employment Subsidy was for a while much relied on, it is now thought that the wage subsidies in fact triggered a competitive wage spiral through the whole industry. As the TES cost about £450 million during its four-year life, which ended in 1979 and affected over half a million people, it is easy to see that a really ambitious jobs-saving scheme also has a major impact on the economy.

This vexed question of leakage and slippage, in which government spending filters rapidly into the economy as a whole and sparks a wages-cost inflationary spiral, is the major argument against many job-creating techniques, and is therefore a recurring theme in the following chapter. But it also provides ammunition for those who urge civilian 'conscription' as a way to tackle the particular problem of youth unemployment.

Michael Emmerson, one of the European Commission's top economists, believes that the leak-proof nature of civilian 'National Service' will ensure that it will join work-sharing and greatly expanded training and educational schemes to make up a three-pronged EEC joblessness strategy during the 1980s. To officials, the idea of being able to scrub large numbers of unemployed young people off the books almost at a stroke must be attractive. Although at first sight the idea looks politically unacceptable, it could no doubt be dressed up in the trappings of a Peace Corps. The image of a motivated youth force occupying itself with vital social service work in the hospitals, amongst the elderly and in the inner-cities, patching up the torn fabric of a Caring Society, could conceivably be made quite attractive. But the blunt reality is, as one UK Department of Employment official put it, that any form of conscription would be seen 'as shit work for lower class kids'.

The leak-proof qualities of youth conscription also raise further political difficulties. Making sure the National Service army of young unemployed is unable to leak money into the wage economy has nothing to do with penning the conscripts up behind the barbed wire of disused camps. It has to do with paying them a good deal less than they might otherwise earn in a real job. In the UK, where the absence of any form of military service if anything enhances the various attractions of civilian service, the pay rates contained in various proposals are considerably less than dole benefits or training schemes offer, let alone average wages. The most detailed plan, put forward by Enrico Colombatto of the London School of Economics with the enthusiastic backing of the LSE's director, Professor Ralf Dahrendorf, suggests a wage of about £10 a week and keep. The Treasury, meanwhile, is baulking at the £2–3 billion that mobilizing an army of the unemployed would probably cost.

Setting extremely low pay rates, that are two-thirds of the dole that a jobless teenager can draw, presumably goes hand-in-hand with a tough decision to coerce school-leavers. It also raises a host of still unanswered questions about how much the glut of young people should earn in work.

Jim Prior, when he was Employment Secretary, worried that young people coming on to the labour market were pricing themselves out of work, and losing ground in the jobs stakes to adult women who are happy to accept part-time employment at highly competitive rates. He believes that there is a need to stabilize wage rates for youth, and those who charge the trades unions with ensuring high youth unemployment through rigid wage structures would agree with him. Interestingly enough, a PA management Consultants' survey of the reasons and prospects for youth unemployment, backed that up not long ago with the finding that many employers had decided to limit or abandon the recruitment of 16–18 year-olds because they are 'poor value for money'. The survey, which was commissioned by the Confederation of British Industry and financed by National Westminster Bank, cited complaints about poor educational standards amongst young jobseekers, and forecast alarming unemployment levels for them by 1983 as one result. The study focused on three areas of the UK to provide a cross section, and found that in the Midlands industrial new town of Redditch as many as 74 per cent of young people may be unemployed by 1983, Preston in north-west England could have a 66 per cent rate of youth unemployment and in the London borough of Southwark the prediction is a 42 per cent level.

Market forces could eventually start to force youth to price itself back into work, but that still does not let governments off the hook of having to face up to the problem of deciding how much young people should earn. In the coming years, governments will, directly and indirectly, become the single largest employers of youth. They will have to set the rates for the several millions of young people throughout Europe who are part of the various make-work, training or subsidy schemes they operate. All will find themselves caught in an impossible crossfire between those who charge that special youth pay rates are an exploitation of the young that is designed to provide employers with cheap labour, and those who claim it is a ploy to undercut and disrupt overall wage rates.

One technique for mopping up teenage unemployment without having to open this Pandora's Box of pay rate squabbles is, of course, training and education. More accurately, governments need only lift the lid a fraction. Keeping youth in the classrooms has much to recommend it, and the money problem is reduced to the more manageable issue of constructing some sort of system, in which dole benefits do not act as a magnet enticing children away from school. One idea in Britain has been to create a single Youth Benefit, a sort of state pocket-money, that would be paid to young people irrespective of whether they are in or out of the labour market.

The attraction of education and training on a vastly increased scale seems clear enough. In political terms it keeps the youthful off the unemployment register, and, by extension, off the police blotter. It also costs less than attempting to construct a whole new administration, such as that required by a conscription system, and has considerably more practical value than any make-work scheme could have.

Some people have reservations about using education as a means of combating the jobs crisis. The authors of the LSE plan for youth conscription apparently considered that it was more important to occupy young people than to educate them, arguing that the latter might encourage ambitions which the labour market cannot fulfil. It seems an odd view for educationalists to hold, although possibly it owes something to the spectre of graduate unemployment that always stalks the Groves of Academe. Indeed, graduate unemployment is a problem in itself. In the UK the rate of new graduates unable to find a job fairly quickly almost doubled between 1970 and 1980 to around nine per cent, rising to a high of 13·5 per cent of men[16] who had read arts subjects. And Italy is often pointed to as a prime example of what is sometimes called 'cultural unemployment' so that its university faculties of literature, jurisprudence and political science were not long ago dubbed by an official report as 'factories of unemployment'.[17] That said, it nevertheless seems a misleading argument, for those slow-starting British graduates numbered just over 5000 and there really is no reason to suppose that in Britain or in Italy education is a lasting handicap in finding a job.

There is, on the contrary, very convincing evidence that lack of education or skills lies at the root of many people's unemployment, and, furthermore, that a national dearth of skills and qualifications will increasingly hold back a country's economic progress and employment prospects. American experts like Peter Drucker are confident that the 'education explosion', which accompanied the baby boom years in the US, will not hold the American economy back. If anything, the problem will be to create 'knowledge jobs' at a fast enough rate to absorb them. But in Europe there are growing doubts over the educational abilities of the workforce and its adaptability to technological revolution, and nowhere does the problem seem more pronounced than in Britain. At one end of the scale university education is being cut back, at the other the country's antique apprenticeship and industrial training system has been revealed as a national disgrace.[18]

Even West German experts worry about the training question, pointing to the fact that two-thirds of all unemployed are totally unskilled, while the proportion of jobs in the labour market requiring no skills is one-third. Yet the German record on training, together with that of all other highly industrialized countries, puts Britain to shame. In France 40 per cent of youths receive full-time vocational training on leaving school, against just 10 per cent in the UK. In Britain, 44 per cent of school-leavers receive no further training of any sort, while for Germany the figure is 6–9 per cent, in France 19 per cent and Italy 23 per cent. There seems no disagreement between industry and government agencies like the Manpower Services Commission that this traditional skills shortage is often acute in vital high technology areas and has for some years prevented Britain from remaining in the vanguard of new growth sectors. Some observers, perhaps the best known being Prince Philip, have suggested that a by-product of recession might well be more training. In fact, the number of school-leavers taking up apprenticeships in the leading industrial cities has dropped by about half since the downturn began.

The link between even the most basic skills-training schemes and greatly improved employment prospects is inescapable. West Germany's vocational training system has an impressive record, with 60 per cent of its intake consisting of youths who were previously unemployed and a subsequent joblessness rate of only five per cent among those who completed the course. Nor does Germany resort to specially low youth wage rates to make the products of such courses potentially more attractive. The European Commission, which advocates an EEC-wide drive on training, is as impressed as most other analysts with German methods and clearly sees them as a model. But, while training is one of the few techniques that do respond well to having large sums of money thrown at them, it seems doubtful that any of the EEC governments are in the mood to throw large sums of money in the direction of the Brussels Commission.

The sort of dent that training and apprentice schemes can make in youth unemployment as it continues its inexorable rise during the 1980s is hard to tell. It depends not only on how much is invested but also on whether more highly skilled workforces prove to have a dynamic quality of their own – so that through being more suited to harness new technology they are more competitive, and so grab a larger slice of international markets and generate more work for themselves. West Germany's likely retention of its huge manufacturing base throughout the 1980s seems to bear that out.

Just as crucial is the expansion of higher education. Although it naturally has a negligible direct effect on unemployment, advanced education provides the driving force to power a skilled workforce. Britain and the rest of Western Europe now risk dropping steadily behind the US and Japan in high technology training and development. The lead the US has already established in biochemical research and genetic engineering, and the dominance of both the Americans and the Japanese in micro-electronic developments, is causing mounting concern in European universities. In the UK, however, that alarm is turning to panic as spending cuts are imposed on universities that could within a decade suppress graduate training and research facilities in key science and engineering areas. Of the 45 universities in Britain it is feared that ten of them could suffer that fate.[19] Even if a reduction of about five per cent in the number of British undergraduates, currently about 235,000 may be seen as an acceptable measure, the effects of such cuts become progressive inside the educational system. As it is, European education on the whole is not supplying industry with enough graduates to satisfy demand in high technology sectors. France is believed to be suffering from a shortage of 20,000 qualified computer specialists, in Italy the deficit is put at 15,000 and in Britain 25,000.[20] That the universities are not turning out enough people with the right scientific qualifications is an old refrain, but it gets no easier on the ear.

Nor does the arithmetic of educational penny-pinching seem to make much sense. In the wake of the British government's 1981 decision to impose cuts totalling £170 million on the country's university system over the following three years, Professor Tom Stonier at Bradford University produced the following calculation. Taking his own university, which will see its budget cut by £2·27 million during that period, he estimated that the 100 staff members to be dismissed would cost an average £10,000 a head in compensation, representing a total of £1 million. To that he added the cost of the 830 cut in Bradford's student population. He reckoned that they would either join the ranks of the unemployed, or ensure that other less adequate youths did, at a cost per head of £5000 to the state rather than the £3000 needed to keep them at university. 'That is another £1·5 million spent', he commented, 'and the savings Bradford is supposed to be making are swallowed up.'[21] He has stressed that his figures are not definitive, and indeed they seem conservative. If his £2000 per student per year 'gap' is valid, the cut in Bradford's student population works out at a shade under £5 million for the three-year period, and for the country as a whole the total is £72 million. While for university teaching job cuts, due to total somewhere between 3000 and 7000, the sums involved become almost astronomical. The University Grants Committee puts the cost of each compulsory redundancy at £40–80,000 so that at its lowest the cost involved would be £120 million, rising to a high of £560 million.[22] In the meantime, at the OECD in Paris specialists in education and youth employment are increasingly anxious that in the UK as elsewhere no research is being carried out into the changes that new technology is already making to the 'occupational structure' of industrial countries. Universities should already be turning out a new generation of teachers capable of tailoring primary and secondary education to the requirements of a post-industrial society.

It sometimes seems that Treasury ministers are like a bunch of enthusiastic but incompetent gardeners, whose financial husbandry consists of snipping off the healthy buds on the economic rosebush and leaving the deadheads.

Certainly, they have problems of their own that an ill-considered public spending splurge could turn from threat to fact. A relapse back into double-digit hyperinflation, or an increase in public debt so sharp that it shattered international confidence in sterling, would create crises so severe that the unemployed would be among the first to suffer. Those are precisely the rocks, the Jeremiahs warn, on which France's reflationary job-promoting strategy will founder. But it is also clear that in Britain, whatever the government chooses to do, it is already committed by the jobs crisis to spending money that the country does not have or cannot afford – the distinction is made unclear by the printing presses of the Royal Mint.

In its spring 1981 *Review of the Economy and Employment* Warwick University's respected Manpower Research Group made the following projections of the UK's public sector debts and therefore borrowing needs. Assuming no dramatic U-turn away from the government's economic objectives, it saw the 1981 Public Sector Borrowing Requirement – the amount needed to balance the government's books – falling from £11·5 billion, or 4·7 per cent of the gross domestic product, right down to £5·1 billion, a mere 1·4 per cent of GDP, by 1985. Unemployment benefit, which according to the Treasury's calculations represents a third of the direct fiscal cost of unemployment, is meanwhile seen as rising from £2·9 billion in 1981 to £4·6 billion in 1985. The twin suggestions appear to be that while over five years the yearly direct cost of joblessness will have risen from £8·7 billion to almost £14 billion (and, if the X4 'opportunity cost' formula were applied, to approaching £60 billion), the pressure on the government's credit position will have eased considerably. Of course it is a commendable piece of economic housekeeping to get Britain so close to being back in the black, but the unemployed might be forgiven for complaining that there is little point in having a clean and shiny kitchen if there is no food on the table.

The choice in any case seems to lie between spending more money on unemployment in the negative sense of pouring it down the dole drain, or using the leeway of otherwise diminishing public debt to combat it actively.

Along with other countries, Britain spends considerably less on all its schemes to promote employment than it does on compensating unemployment. Even counting in, as one should, the controversial bail-out funds being handed over at a yearly rate of about £2 billion to save jobs at BL, British Steel and British Shipbuilders, other job subsidy measures and manpower schemes of all types bring the combined total of 'positive' spending to no more than the £4 billion a year mark; less than half the money being spent on 'negative' benefits.

Why not, then, introduce a new system under which the government employs the unemployed? In the same way that Roosevelt's 'New Deal' of the 1930s transferred America's Great Depression victims from the 'Hoovervilles' in which they were encamped around the soup kitchens into a vast public works programme that undertook valuable infrastructural work. Or at any rate, why not harness some of the energies of the unemployed through social services programmes and at least see some return on the taxpayers' benefits outlay? Such, increasingly, are the noises being made in many of the industrial countries. Unfortunately, putting people on to the government payroll is not that simple, for most of the techniques that might be used turn out to be political minefields.

The most straightforward method is the US 'workfare' idea, where people work for their welfare payments. It is being pushed as a national measure by President Reagan, and in some parts of America like Cincinnati, Ohio, it has been practised for the last 40 years. The scheme requires recipients of welfare to put in an average of about twenty hours a month in part-time labour that can range from helping run a creche for small children to a spot of municipal gardening. In late 1980 the voters of San Diego County, California, overwhelmingly adopted the idea, and since then it has been operating as a pilot scheme, with interestingly mixed results. Some of the women drawn into 'workfare' were grateful for the chance to become involved in social service work, but the most marked trend was the number of people who refused to turn up to do their workfare job.

Ronald Reagan has claimed that 'workfare' provides 'valuable training and self-esteem', yet the indications are that people reject it because of its compulsory and 'make-work' nature. In the San Diego County project, only 440 of the 1700 people required to do their twenty hours of work a month ever showed up. It was, in fact, surprising that the voters there opted 9–1 to implement the scheme, for there already existed evidence that 'workfare' is obstinately resisted by people on welfare. When Reagan was Governor of California in the early 1970s, similar work conditions were imposed in 35 of the state's 58 counties. But less than 10,000 people out of a potential taskforce calculated at 2 million ever did any community service work. In a report analysing 'workfare', California's Employment Development Department later made it plain that, in addition to massive unwillingness of welfare recipients to be forced into work, the difficulties of administering such a scheme were a big limiting factor.[23]

Much more sophisticated than 'workfare', and much more politically acceptable because there is no element of coercion, are the various proposals being put forward in Europe for using unemployment benefits to fund jobs. The government in effect cuts its losses by recognizing that, whatever happens, it will be supporting anyone who is registered as unemployed, and so it transfers that money to an employer as a wage subsidy. In a quiet way that has already been happening in Britain, for the Community Enterprise Programme, operated by the Manpower Services Commission at a cost of almost £80 million in 1981, has been funding co-operatives and training workshops, and so transferring the youthful and long-term unemployed in a positive way from one government budget to another. Perhaps the most striking illustration of how effective the technique can be on a small scale has been provided by a Danish fishing village in north Jutland. Almost 40 per cent of Denmark's eight per cent unemployment rate is made up of under-25s, and in the depressed fishing port of Hanstholm the proportion was higher still. The town council there tackled the problem by using the benefits that would have been paid to the unemployed to create a new manufacturing operation from scratch.

Hanstholm set about producing the wooden crates used to box fish. These had previously been bought in from outside, but, by making 80,000 crates in the first year, the village was able to supply its own needs and 'export' a surplus to neighbouring villages. In addition to diverting benefit payments to help fund the operation, Hanstholm also put an extra two per cent on the local rates. But school-leavers now have work at a union-agreed wage, and as well as crate-making a variety of community jobs are also available.[24]

The ideal, therefore, is to construct a system so straightforward yet flexible that it can be applied in a wide variety of conditions as an encouragement for employers to take on more labour. Professor Richard Layard, of the LSE's Centre for Labour Economics, has proposed a scheme whose hallmark is brilliant simplicity. That is important because the sheer range and complexity of the different manpower schemes now being operated discourages employers with the bureaucratic red tape it entails. Layard's suggestion was that, as the direct Exchequer cost of an unemployed person averages £70-a-week, the government should undertake to pay that amount to any employer who hires for at least a year someone who has already been on the dole for six months or more. The only condition attached is that naturally the employer must be making a net increase in the size of his labour force. Apart from the claim that it could quickly generate over quarter of a million new jobs, the scheme has other attractions. It is more economical than any direct public sector employment scheme would be – Samuel Brittan, the *Financial Times'* economics commentator has calculated that, for the state to employ the jobless at similar zero net cost, it could only pay such unattractively low rates as £30 per week for a single man and £60 for a married man with two children – yet it is sufficient, when topped up by the employer, not to provoke trade union opposition to wage rate under-cutting.

The arguments over the precise effect of such schemes are interminable and inconclusive. The British government is currently opting for another version of Professor Layard's idea, which is aimed particularly at making school-leavers more attractive to employers, and which combines low pay rates with subsidies granted through National Insurance relief. This method is said to ensure that no inflationary wage spirals will be created, which means presumably that the unions will view it as a disruptive gambit to de-stabilize wages through exploiting 'child labour'. Certainly there seem few if any techniques for tinkering with the labour market that are not accused by detractors of having some serious drawback or other. Even the notion of offering early retirement inducements, to make room inside the labour market for new entrants, is not immune to this sniping, although in Denmark it was reckoned during 1979–80 to have reduced the joblessness rate to five per cent when it would otherwise have been at seven per cent.

There are a number of broad conclusions that can nevertheless be drawn. The first is that, as unemployment worsens, governments will anyway be forced to spend more, and will no doubt find it preferable to be seen to be doing something, however cosmetic. That in itself moves the emphasis from funding the dole drain to undertaking much more visible schemes. The second is that, as the projections in Chapter 2 made clear beyond any reasonable doubt, during the years of the 1980s there is no foreseeable power on earth that can generate enough real peacetime jobs to satisfy demand enough to keep OECD joblessness down at around 25 million people. Therefore jobs must be created that are not real work. The tactic of keeping people off the register should only be viewed as a dodge when governments use it to avoid facing the reality of the jobs crisis.

9

Job Creation and Construction

A puzzled Jobs Marcher said it all. Drenched to the skin by a mid-May downpour and footsore as he trudged along through the suburbs of Birmingham, the redundant joiner explained to a reporter from *The Times* why he and so many others on the 1981 People's March for Jobs were genuinely baffled.

How was it, he asked, that so many building workers were unemployed when tens of thousands of families were badly housed?[1]

It is a question that cuts through much of the peripheral debate about making less work go farther, and through a good deal of the economic theorizing that risks becoming an alibi for inaction. Britain, no less than all other industrialized countries, does not lack work to be done. Housing is in chronic shortage and by the mid-80s will be in crisis, while the infrastructure of roads, rail transport and power supply, that so strongly influences industrial costs, is overdue for improvement. Rectifying these deficiencies is not making work, it is instead using work, that should be done, to create real and lasting jobs. With the important added advantage that the projects for which there is a genuine need neatly match many of the most urgent unemployment blackspots. Action against inner-city blight, for example, provides local employment and could stop the rot of ghetto rioting.

A determined drive to improve neglected and outmoded parts of the UK economic engine would create not just hundreds of thousands of new jobs but possibly several million, and would, furthermore, probably pay for itself sooner rather than later.

But, before examining in more detail how and why it should be done, it is as well first to hear the case for the opposition, for there are limiting factors too.

Oh no, chorus the critics, you can't just stimulate the economy with public works programmes. That's demand management, Keynesian pump-priming, and, although it will create some jobs in the short term, it will in the longer run spark serious inflation that will lead to the suppression not just of those new jobs but of many others as well. Indeed there is, in normal times, a fairly direct trade-off between unemployment and inflation. It is well known that an increase in joblessness is usually accompanied by a decrease in inflation. That, notoriously, was why most ministers in the Thatcher government observed rising unemployment in the early days after they took office with some equanimity. Furthermore, because of that seesaw effect between unemployment and inflation, there is a notional point at which the two can be in balance – in the jargon it is called full employment equilibrium, or the 'natural' rate of joblessness at which inflation will be frozen.

When inflation is identified as Economic Enemy No. 1, as it has been until very recently by almost all governments in the Western industrialized countries, unemployment is seen as the logical lever for pushing it back down again. To a large extent it works. There have been disconcerting departures from the rule in recent years, beginning in the late 1960s when it was found that sluggish economies could nevertheless be plagued by high inflation, in a phenomenon that was variously nicknamed 'stagflation' or 'slumpflation'. But in general terms the relationship holds good. The trouble is that nobody has been able to measure the way in which it works, or even agree on the detail of why it works. As a result, there is considerable doubt about the extent to which it works, and the room for manoeuvre that exists in which greater employment can be encouraged without triggering hyper-inflation.

For a while, about twenty years ago, some economists thought they could measure the workings of the jobs-inflation scales. It was quite quickly found that they could not and the experts have been arguing about it ever since.

In November 1958 an economist named A. W. Phillips caused something of a stir in academic circles, when he published a paper in the journal *Economica* apparently proving the direct link between employment levels and wage settlements that were high enough to be inflationary. Researching back over almost 100 years to 1861 he was able to demonstrate that low unemployment and high pay rates went tightly hand-in-hand. Thus was born the celebrated 'Phillips Curve', a seemingly useful formula for using the dole queue as an instrument of economic management. It was not in fact a novel approach by any means, but it has retained considerable political respectability long after Phillips and his curve were torn to shreds by other economists.

The first thing wrong with Phillips' formula was that it analysed economic behaviour of a byegone age. It worked just fine, the experts said, during the years up to the outbreak of World War I, when there really was a free market in labour and governments had not yet begun to rig the market by making deals on the side with trade unions and employers.[2] But the sharpest blow to the Curve's credibility came when it was just ten years old as an economic theory. Trade unions throughout Europe and in North America pressed home extremely inflationary wage demands even though joblessness was on the rise.

Of course, many of the other criticisms levelled against Phillips hold good too, for the whole idea that inflation and full employment are quite irreconcilable – and that therefore there is a political dilemma in which governments must choose one or the other. The first is that even high unemployment, perhaps up to ten per cent or so, attacks first and foremost the unskilled and less adequate workers. They are the ones with the least trades union clout because they are most easily replaced, and are not anyway doing the sort of qualified work that most effectively holds an employer to ransom with a threatened stoppage.

Unemployment would need to be at catastrophically high levels before the highly skilled trades would be bludgeoned into accepting losses in real income. Britain's experience since 1979 rather bears the point out; overall pay settlements have been lower, but not nearly as low as the unemployment figures might have suggested they would be. There is also an interesting theory now being put forward in the United States that unemployment, far from being a handy instrument for combating inflation, instead fuels it. Lester Thurow summed up the argument in the columns of the *New York Times* not long ago. 'Recessions and unemployment may provide a short-run cure for inflation', he wrote, 'but they make the long-run problem worse. Because training has been halted during the previous recession, the economy runs out of skilled blue-collar workers even faster in the next economic boom. And as companies bid for the limited supply of skilled blue-collar workers, inflation breaks out even sooner and more virulently than it did in the previous economic boom.'[3]

What much of this boils down to is that although there is a crude interplay between employment and inflation, it is by no means clear-cut enough to discredit investment programmes as a means of creating new jobs, providing that a couple of simple, commonsense rules are observed. The first is to embark only on projects that are genuinely necessary and can be judged to be a sound investment, preferably in commercial terms but certainly in overall economic advantage to the country. Money invested in, say, the construction of a power station clearly works straight through into large areas of the private sector as a source of sub-contracts, and ultimately means that industry will be able to buy its power more cheaply. Paying teenagers to clear up a beach, on the other hand, may be socially desirable but in economic terms just means that wages are being paid without any marketable product. Beach cleaning is a local government service, not an investment.

The second rule, which follows naturally from the first, is that the relationship between output and wages should be more rigorously controlled than has generally been the case. In other words, governments should insist that the ground rule for new investment programmes is that productivity increases must be better than the norm. Having created a new market for work, they are entitled to impose conditions, and, politically sensitive as that may be, it helps ensure that government funds do not merely fuel inflation. The bulk of unemployed labour that would be attracted to the new projects is in any case made up of manual workers at the lower-skilled end of the market, who are more malleable than strongly unionized craftsmen, and should anyway be grateful for work, providing the strings attached are not wholly unreasonable.

The best system might be for new projects funnelling public money into the economy to be marshalled under a tough new overlord authority, since it would be important to set sub-contract prices at levels that demand similar productivity improvements from suppliers. The idea of 'take it or leave it' contract work, at prices that industry will cavil at, may sound shocking, but work-hungry companies would themselves find it a valuable underpinning as they attempt to negotiate wage moderation.

In Britain, the launching of yet another state authority would at first, no doubt, be greeted with understandable scepticism. But, for housing alone, the sheer scale of work that needs to be done, and the volume of real and profitable employment that could be generated, argues powerfully for a centralized body empowered to cut through the delays and inconsistencies of local authority management. Treasury officials, who themselves see both immediate and long term advantages in a housing drive, also warn that the subject is a sacred cow to both major political parties, while to the present government a national authority might well be political anathema.

Leaving aside organizational squabbles, the fundamental argument is the unused potential of housing for a major lift-off of employment and economic activity. It would not just be in the construction industry, but in a range of hard-pressed sectors such as timber, bricks, cement, glass, furniture and pottery, not to mention textiles and steel where a pick-up in orders could make the difference between life and death for some companies or production units. German analysis now suggests that the construction industry's share of the cost of a house is only 32 per cent, with the remaining 68 per cent accounted for indirectly in sub-contracts.[4] In rough terms, that means that, for each new building worker put to work, another two industrial jobs would be created or at least saved.

Creating jobs on building sites would in itself be extremely attractive without that industrial bonus. Construction industry workers are many of them poorly skilled, and are among the least likely to find work again as the jobs crisis deepens. In the construction industries of Britain, France, West Germany and Italy alone, the EEC's Big Four, there are estimated to be up to three-quarters to one million jobless with the UK accounting for over 400,000 of that total.

Industry's vanishing markets have been one of the chief underlying causes of the new unemployment, and have had much to do with employers' inability to absorb the jobseekers of the baby boom generation. Yet housing throughout Europe and the United States – to say nothing of Japan and its famous 'rabbit hutches' – represents a huge and unsatisfied market. In the US, only one in ten of all potential first-time home buyers is now able to afford to become an owner-occupier, and the vicious circle of inflation and the slow down of construction has since 1974 pushed prices up by an impossible 82 per cent-plus.[5] In Holland, and even in rich, complacent Switzerland, housing shortages are severe enough to have caused serious youth rioting. In West Germany, the cost of a home in relation to incomes is more than double that in the UK, so ownership remains the preserve of a privileged minority.

In France, where one of the first actions of the new government was to boost planned house construction in both 1981 and 1982 from 350,000 units in each year to 450,000, there remains a worryingly high proportion of dilapidated houses that also need urgent improvement, and the same goes for Belgium.

But it is in the UK that there probably exists the greatest scope and need for a housing boom. The early spending cuts introduced by the Thatcher government, doubtless because they were the most easily realized ones, have now produced a rapidly widening gap between supply and demand for public housing, that by 1986 will mean a crisis shortage of nearly 1 million homes. There is another crucially important aspect to housing, and it concerns the mobility of British workers. Employers rightly complain that this immobility leads to acute regional labour shortages – only one per cent of the UK working population moves house for job or training reasons. But it is scarcely surprising, when shortages force local authorities to operate priority list systems, and when rent controls have during the past ten years led to the disappearance of one-third of all privately rented housing.[6] It is essential to solve the mobility problem, for it lies at the root of wasteful mismatch, in which a skilled worker may be mouldering unproductively on the dole in town A, while not far away in town B there are unfilled vacancies for his particular craft. By the same token, enforced immobility produced by over-tight housing conditions is already confounding the best efforts of the present government to operate a more effective regional development policy.

Before examining the direct economic advantages of a drive on house construction and other types of infrastructural investment, it is worth taking a closer look at the hidden drawbacks of insufficient housing. Although American workers are frequently held up as a model of mobility, US employers are now also complaining that the workforce has become rooted in traditional industrial areas and is holding back expansion elsewhere.

Despite the strong population shift toward the West Coast and the 'sunbelt' states of the south-west – America's population centre, the point of balance between eastern and western populations, was found in the 1980 census to have moved west across the Mississippi river for the first time – labour shortages stemming from immobility have become an important factor. Regional economies in the US have since the mid-1970s developed at very different rates, and one result has been that property prices in California can average three times the going rate in depressed 'snowbelt' traditional industrial states such as Michigan or Ohio. Many prime skilled workers can no longer afford to move to where the jobs are.

In Europe, regional attachments are on the whole stronger and have also been reinforced by the trend towards devolution that was such a marked feature of politics in many European countries during the latter 1970s. But, whatever the attractions of being identified as a Chouan from France's Vendée or a Welshman from the valleys, the need to work is fast becoming a more powerful imperative. Both Chouan and Welshman, however, are locked into systems of regionally watertight public housing in which there is no efficient mechanism for swapping accommodation. In Britain, housing experts believe that in order to allow true mobility of the workforce, the surplus of housing, known as the 'vacancy reserve', would need to be of the order of ten per cent, which in turn means that an extra 2 million homes would be required.[6] In France, probably about another 1 million.

The Thatcher government in the UK is increasingly coming down on the side of mobility as the key to regional development, although it does not appear to have grasped that its own slashing of public housing construction programmes is already hamstringing such a policy. In the age-old debate over whether government should take the jobs to the people or the people to the jobs, Sir Keith Joseph, the then Industry Secretary, was, shortly before his translation to Education Secretary, making it clear that he favoured the latter approach. And not without reason.

In his confidential report to the National Economic Development Council in April, 1981, Sir Keith challenged the wisdom of continuing to support chronically ailing areas of the UK beset by high unemployment and saddled with the structural problems of outmoded industries. 'After spending large sums of money – for example some £5 billion since 1971 – the areas in greatest need in the thirties remain the areas of greatest need now', he pointed out in his memorandum. 'Why this is so, despite the policies designed to redress the balance between the poorer and the relatively more prosperous areas of the country, is something of an enigma and leads inevitably to the question of whether the money spent in the past could not have been better spent. More importantly, should we still be subsidizing these areas now?' On balance, Sir Keith Joseph clearly thought not, and the jobs record of Britain's regional policies rather supports his view. The Department of Industry says that, from 1971–76, the three entirely-assisted regions of Scotland, Wales and the North of England together achieved only 11,000 gross new jobs on average every year. Considering the speed with which other jobs have been going under in those regions, the Department was almost certainly understating the position when it added, 'The net employment effect will have been considerably smaller.'[7]

When the Thatcher government came to power in May 1979, 44 per cent of Britain's working population was in assisted areas, so that the concept of regional development was being spread so thin as to risk being meaningless. By 1982, that proportion is being shrunk to just 25 per cent, which seems to make a good deal more sense. But, if the government's plan is that workers should begin to move away from some of the abandoned assisted areas, it would be sound to look at how in practice that can be stymied by the realities of the housing shortage. Worse, the situation has been made even more difficult by the present government's own spending cuts. In house construction, of course, but also in a valuable and comparatively inexpensive removal and re-location scheme operated by the Manpower Services Commission, which has been cut in half.

Two instructive examples of how housing is the crucial element in tackling the regional mismatch question are worth considering. In mid-79 employers in the Norfolk town of King's Lynn were faced with 160 apparently unfillable vacancies for skilled jobs, and turned to the unemployment blackspot of South Shields to solve the problem. The employment services there responded promptly and a coachload of 52 jobseekers, half of them accompanied by wives, arrived for a tour of the area and job interviews. Twenty-five of those men accepted work offers and moved south to King's Lynn, because the local council had cut red tape to make 60 houses available over six months. As a King's Lynn employment adviser commented afterwards of the scheme's success, 'Without housing it would not have been worth mounting.' Conversely, a lack of housing has cost other towns with skill shortages dearly. Medway in Kent took the trouble to bring 24 skilled Scottish workers down from Kilmarnock without similar provision being made for housing them. While thirteen eventually took jobs down south, a Medway employment official observed, 'Had the housing been available I am sure that 24 jobs would have been filled.'[8]

Ironing out mismatch must be made a top priority, for, if unemployment in general is an economic waste, failure to employ all available skills is a form of industrial suicide. Mismatch naturally enough does not affect the unskilled as they have nothing to offer that would be in short supply elsewhere. The notified vacancies in Britain underscore the point, for nine-tenths of the 120,000 unfilled jobs registered with the employment services are for jobs with varying degrees of skill. It is usually reckoned that for each notified vacancy there are in fact two more that go unregistered. So the sorry picture that emerges is one of joblessness among the skilled that has lately been increasing at twice the national rate, while more than 350,000 skilled jobs are at any given moment going begging in Britain. It seems short-sighted, to put it mildly, for the government to have cut the MSC's Employment Transfer Scheme, which in 1979 helped move 10,000 key workers at a cost of £7 million, to only £4 million a year, at a time when the mismatch problem is growing.

As errors go, it is as nothing to the folly of axing public housing construction, which is the mainspring of activity in the building industry. Three-quarters of the Conservative government's total spending cut-backs fell on house construction, with the result that, with only 56,000 building 'starts' in the public sector in both 1980 and 1981, Britain's public housing programme is running at a somewhat lower total than, say, Sweden's. More to the point, the gap between needs and available housing in both the public and private sectors is widening fast. Every year in Britain 180,000 new households are formed, while, together with the 97,000 private sector house starts currently being made by the building industry, new houses are being provided at the rate of just over 150,000 a year. But that apparent shortfall of 30,000 homes very much understates the position. Out of the total 20 million dwellings that make up the UK housing stock, at least one per cent needs to be replaced every year because of age and dilapidation. Even that one per cent is considered by housing experts to be woefully inadequate, but it happens to be the rate that government spending considerations and fiscal policies for the private sector have more or less dictated. All in all, it is reckoned that the UK can just about scrape by if 300,000 new homes are built every year – double the present level – but that 380,000 would be a much sounder target.

That is without taking any account of the need for more houses to promote labour mobility. A vacancy reserve of the order of ten per cent mentioned earlier would have to be borne by the public sector, for private owners, in the words of one senior building society executive, would not be able to afford the 'philanthropy' of so much empty property. At present, the UK has on paper a 4·6 per cent vacancy reserve, but that figure is widely recognized as being phoney because it includes a great deal of unusable property. To reach that ten per cent reserve the public housing stock would need to be boosted from 6 million dwellings to 8 million. At current average public housing prices of £30,000 per house and £20,000 per flat that adds up to £40–60 billion. But would it be a cost to the economy or a boost?

Rather more than 870,000 new homes will anyway be needed in Britain by 1986 at a cost of around £25 billion at current (1981) prices. With public housing running at about a third of all construction, the Treasury can think in terms of allocating over £8 billion for the government's share. Thinking in those cost terms, however, is misleading in a country where, as Chapter 8 showed, the deadweight cost of unemployment is probably close to £40 billion a year. Apart from land, which represents only a sixth of the cost of building a house, money spent on construction will be channelled straight into building site employment and industrial activity.

If governments chose to be truly imaginative, though, it would be possible to provide much of this boost to demand without it even appearing, for a while, as a charge on the public ledger. New mortgage systems, such as one that is being urged by economists at the Massachusetts Institute of Technology, could rapidly bring house purchasing within the grasp of millions, and so bring about the re-birth of activity in private sector house construction. Labour mobility would be greatly aided, and public housing could be concentrated more on real need in the inner-cities.

It says much of the hidebound nature of government and financial institutions that the ingenious method of reducing the 'front end loading' of interest payments on a mortgage, devised by Professor Franco Modigliani at MIT, has attracted little interest since it was first proposed to the White House in 1977. Yet its basic objective, of smoothing out repayments to match the disposable income of the average child-rearing couple, would revolutionize demand for home ownership. In Britain, surveys have shown that, although only a shade over half of all households are owner-occupiers, at least 70 per cent aspire to be.[9] In West Germany, where a house usually costs eight times the average annual income, as against 3·3 times in the UK, and where the financing system is by British standards 'unwieldy', the degree of untapped demand is probably higher still. The caution of governments might be understandable, for Modigliani's scheme would require either fiscal or financial help during the early years before it could span two generations of buyers. But the financial institutions' lack of interest in a short cut to much more business is puzzling.

Named, not very euphoniously, 'the Constant Payment Factor Variable Rate Mortgage', the Modigliani method amounts to a more flexible and polished version of such variants as the 'balloon' mortgage and the 'purchasing power' mortgage that is much used in economies with chronic hyper-inflation, like Israel. Modigliani's mortgage aims first of all to avoid demanding high initial repayments, something that is known in the technical argot as the 'tilt' problem. In simple terms, he explains, a home buyer borrows 100 units on a traditional mortgage, and, if inflation is so low as to be close to zero, he would repay that amount at a constant rate of five or six units a year over 30 years. That would be very satisfactory, but, as inflation never is around zero, what actually happens is that a heavy concentration of interest has to be paid off during the early years of the mortgage, when a young couple's financial commitments elsewhere are liable to be at their highest. The repayments begin to reduce progressively, often at the point when the couple starts to have ample cash to spare – in what American demographers have preciously called the 'empty nest' years.

The indexed, or purchasing power, mortgage goes some way towards solving the problem by revaluing both the repayment and the principal sum owed once a year on the basis of the cost-of-living indices. Thus, if five units on a mortgage of 100 are repaid in the first year, and in the second year inflation is at ten per cent the repayment during that year is 5½ units, and so on. The system is fine for the borrower but unattractive to lenders. The exact opposite is true of variable rates systems, for they combine the tilt problem, that so discourages house buyers, with interest rate hiccups that for many people spell financial disaster. Modigliani's answer is as follows. Starting with a standard mortgage transaction in which five units are repayable in the first year on the 100 borrowed, a variable interest rate contract is also agreed between the borrower and the lender. Broadly, this would consist of the inflation rate plus a debiting rate such as one of the short term market rates.

The mortgage is then adjusted in the light of what that rate turned out to be. The five units of repayment during the first year, which in a standard mortgage would have been swelled by ten per cent inflation to around fifteen units, are only slightly increased in a Modigliani mortgage. For the effects of inflation are spread across both the repayments and the size of the principal that is owed. Thus the borrower might repay only seven units in that year, while the capital sum is increased to 110 units. In reality, though, the capital sum is not really increasing at that rate because it is being depreciated by inflation.[10]

The detailed workings of this new system, or similar designs aimed at overcoming tilt at the start of a mortgage that is greatly worsened by double-digit inflation, are outside the scope of this book. But the important point is that use of such techniques could reverse the present unsatisfactory situation where neither the banker nor the buyer are well served. Take California, the apogee of property profitability, where a house in the Los Angeles suburb of Bel Air in 1973 cost just over $70,000 and now sells for more than half a million dollars. The Hollywood dream of California's flourishing real estate market in fact masks a dispiriting truth. The Golden State's banks have been blaming their lacklustre financial performances on mortgage portfolios that are now 'under water' because they yield less than they cost to fund.[11] Yet those same banks reckon that only about ten per cent of California households can now afford to buy a medium-priced home there with conventional financing.[12] The result is that in the US, as in California, house construction is currently running at only half-speed; housing starts, or new buildings, total about 1 million a year while the number of potential buyers, who would until quite recently have been able to afford to become owner-occupiers, is increasing at a yearly rate of 2 million. That does not count the many millions of others in America who have traditionally been denied home ownership by the hurdle of tilt at the start of a standard mortgage, but who would probably have little difficulty in paying off a loan structured along Modigliani's lines.

If America's difficulties are bad, it goes almost without saying that Britain's are worse. House construction in the UK has now slumped to its lowest peacetime level since 1924–5. Government spending on housing is at about a third of the level of the mid-1970s, with less than £2·25 billion (at 1980 prices) due to be spent in 1983–4. Yet the case for boosting employment through meeting the country's housing needs has been made often enough, and was presented yet again in lucid terms in mid-1981 by one of the construction industry's chiefs. Depressingly enough, he was at the same time complaining bitterly of local authorities' delays in releasing land which were delaying private sector house starts.

Caught between the policy cut-backs of central government and the bureaucratic practices of local government, Lynn Wilson, President of the House-Builders Federation had this to say: 'Every new house built will provide two and a half jobs a year if those directly employed in construction and other related materials and service industries are added together.' He was explaining that, were it not for councils' delays in releasing land, a further 50,000 house starts could have been made in 1981 in addition to the 97,000 mentioned earlier in this chapter. Had private builders been able to go ahead, he pointed out, an extra 125,000 jobs would have been created 'at no cost to the government. It would require no subsidy, it would generate rate revenues for local authorities and it would be largely import free.'[13] That last point is vital, for one of the most attractive aspects of a housing boom is that although increased prosperity would naturally increase peripheral imports, in the shape of consumer goods being bought by the newly re-employed for instance, it is almost solely domestic industry that benefits. Few of the bulky materials involved in house construction would still be competitively priced if imported.

Holland, like France, has already concluded that a housing drive is a fast track to jobs and economic revitalization. From 85,000 starts in 1980 it is spurting ahead to 127,000 in 1981 and thereafter. Taking demolitions into account, the Dutch will put up 1 million net new homes by 1990. That means, proportionately, new housing construction at five times the planned British rate.

In industrialized societies which have come to pride themselves on their quality of life, the option of being able to combine renewed industrial demand with further improvements in living conditions should be doubly attractive. Even without tackling housing needs or the issue of labour immobility, modernizations and energy-saving conversions could anyway provide substantial amounts of work in most European countries. West Germany's post-war housing rush, much of it apartment buildings, produced a high proportion of shoddily constructed blocks that are increasingly expensive to maintain. In France almost a quarter of the population is considered to be living in over-crowded conditions. Before embarking on his well-known investigation of the microchip's future impact, France's economic diagnostician Simon Nora looked into the country's housing problem. In 1975 the Nora-Eveno Report found that the cost of modernizing the country's crumbling housing to 'socially acceptable' standards would run at about half a billion pounds a year.

Paying for housing, both in improvements and new construction, is without doubt a problem. Although governments would quite rapidly find their investment paying off in the form of rising tax receipts and plummeting unemployment costs, the start-up funding has to come to a large degree from the public purse. European Commission officials believe, however, that France and West Germany showed the way to other EEC governments when in April 1981 they announced that they would jointly tap the international capital market for a $6 billion loan to finance job creation and energy-saving investments. For the Bonn government it was a highly innovative and significant move, as West Germany had never before raised funds on the international markets. The view from Brussels is increasingly that all EEC governments should use their combined Community muscle to borrow advantageously in order to invest in jobs.

If Britain were to adopt the comparatively modest target of building half a million new homes a year, rather than the present dangerously inadequate level of 150,000, employment might well increase by almost 900,000 people. Over half a million of those new jobs would be either in manufacturing industry or equally hard-hit 'heavy' service sectors like road haulage or the railways. The cost of the housing drive would set the government back about £8·75 billion (at early '80s prices) to begin with, but that money would at the same time be giving a formidable boost to some of the country's most depressed industries and regions.

Putting all the job-creating eggs into the construction industry's basket is not the complete answer to the problem. Building has the advantage that it can be accelerated fast; and it feeds business directly into the myriad of small companies that make up the industry and so avoids the bottlenecks caused by big companies and more sophisticated projects. But it is generally argued, by those who advocate demand management policies as an antidote to joblessness, that construction should be complemented by other types of government spending. The Labour Party-controlled UK Association of Metropolitan Authorities produced a jobs blueprint in July 1981 that saw housing account for only a third of the total programme. The association urged a £2 billion a year increase in local authorities capital expenditure, with a third of that to be spent on building an extra 100,000 houses a year and the remainder on infrastructure projects such as transport and land reclamation. The total package would in fact cost £6 billion in the first year, as it included a further £1 billion for investment in public corporations and £3 billion as the cost of abolishing the National Insurance surcharge as an additional stimulatory measure. The association claimed that its plan would cut unemployment by 300,000 people, and although it would add £4 billion to the government's 1982–3 borrowing requirement and £3 billion more in 1983–4 it said that the net effect on inflation by early 1984 would be a rise of less than a half per cent.

It sounds expensive, perhaps, but the point to bear in mind when assessing such schemes is that job saving is cheaper than job creation.

If anything, the local authorities' blueprint is too conservative. Infrastructural work is crucial, but by its very nature requires time before projects can be set in motion. During that time more and more jobs are steadily being lost in industry, which are more costly to recreate than to subsidize. What is needed is a judicious mixture of fast working demand stimulation, such as building work, and more durable longer term projects such as railway electrification and modernisation. A housing boom can provide the initial lift-off in a great many industries, while infrastructural and engineering projects will later provide sustained activity in a number of key sectors.

Looking at job creation on that broader base inevitably raises the question of whether much of the jobs crisis could be defused simply by generally reflating the economy – pumping in government funds and introducing tax breaks to encourage business and therefore swell companies' payrolls. For a variety of reasons, there is general agreement amongst most experts that overall reflation is not the answer. It is an attractive idea that, by increasing the temperature inside the greenhouse, all the plants would thrive in the more tropical climate. But in fact many of the temperate varieties would only grow at a moderate rate, while the hothouse atmosphere would mean rampant inflation. Throwing money indiscriminately at job creation is anyway not the technique for getting what Americans call 'the best bang for your buck', and indeed it quickly reaches a saturation point after which it is unprofitable. A recent comparative study of West German and Swedish attempts to stimulate job creation through positive and selective measures made the point forcibly. During the late 1970s, Sweden was spending money on jobs at five times the rate of Germany, but to comparatively little greater advantage. In 1978, a huge 2·5 per cent of Sweden's GNP was going into measures that helped provide employment for 3·65 per cent of the country's labour force. West Germany, meanwhile, was devoting only 0·5 per cent of its GNP to the same sort of schemes, yet was reaching 2·18 per cent of the labour force. A much better bang for the Deutschemark.[14]

The answer is highly selective demand management, the stimulation of tightly targeted sectors, with the aim of making them thrive while preventing inflation from spilling over into the rest of the economy – cloches for individual plants rather than a greenhouse approach. That is precisely the technique the new French government plans to use, but it is easier said than done. Quite apart from the difficulties of avoiding a competitive wages spiral as the workers in other industries fight to stay even or maybe ahead of those in one that is being stimulated, there are political pitfalls. A carefully planned exercise in demand management takes time, if increased production and improved productivity are to mesh neatly together to produce solid, non-inflationary growth. Time is one thing that the French government does not have, for it needs the political impact from more jobs to satisfy expectations both at home and abroad. Resisting pressures to spend money dramatically but more indiscriminately is liable to be one of Prime Minister Pierre Mauroy's hardest tasks.

Exactly which industrial sectors to choose, though, and which types of company to encourage, is far from clear. It is an extraordinary fact, but, 200 years after the Industrial Revolution, the industrialized countries still have only a hazy idea of how the job creation process works. That it usually did work was enough. American analysts are now trying to understand what really took place in the US during the 1970s, when the baby boom generation forced the single largest job creation campaign ever undertaken by a developed economy. America's experience provides Europe, now that it is in similar straits, with some valuable lessons. The US managed during that decade to provide almost exactly the same 10 million net new jobs that Europe now needs in the 1980s. But the list of 'don'ts', resulting from an examination of what was really happening beneath the surface of the American jobs boom, is unfortunately much longer than the list of 'do's'.

The first determined attempt to put under the microscope the nation's extraordinary achievement of coping with a 25 per cent increase in the labour force, which involved the creation during the seventies of about 19 million gross new jobs, was published in 1979. In a study called 'The Job Generation Process', David Birch of the Massachusetts Institute of Technology began by demolishing a number of the assumptions that had for years been unquestioned lynchpins of regional development policies around the world. Companies do not migrate, he found, so there is no point in trying financial inducements either to make them move or stay put. Furthermore, job losses throughout the United States occurred at a more or less standard rate. State by state he found that eight per cent of all jobs were disappearing every year, so that, over a fairly short time span like five years, 40 per cent of all jobs were going under and being replaced by new ones. Those two findings alone shed new light on the debate raging, then as now, over the decline of the 'snowbelt' manufacturing states of the north east and midwest and the rise of the 'sunbelt' states of the west and south-west. Industry was not moving away from the snowbelt, it was just growing much faster in the sunbelt.[15]

In simple terms, Birch was saying that government spending cannot be used to any great advantage in badly depressed regions – jobs evaporate inexorably, yet employers do not actually desert to move elsewhere. It can only be used to increase the rate at which new jobs are created in a growth region, or to make one growth region slightly more attractive than another. It sounds tough on traditional manufacturing centres, but it means that Canute-like regional policies to protect the most battered ones are not just expensive but ineffectual.

So where did America's millions of new jobs come from? The answer is from small, new companies starting up in only a modest way. Of the 7 million net new jobs created in the US between 1969–76, only thirteen per cent were thanks to companies with more than 500 people already on the payroll. As for the 'Fortune 500', the cream of American capitalism, the 500 largest domestic and multi-national corporations, they provided a tiny 2–3 per cent of those much needed jobs.

Young companies, businesses just starting out, accounted for 80 per cent of all the new jobs, and they were inevitably small companies too. Two-thirds of the new employment was provided by concerns with fewer than twenty employees. Birch found that, whereas larger companies in an uncertain economic environ-

194 World Out of Work

ment are 50 per cent more likely to shrink than to grow, smaller companies that survive a very high 'infant mortality rate' are four times more likely to grow than to contract. In the depressed north eastern states of the US, he found that these small companies had accounted for *all* the new jobs created during those years.

David Birch reached two conclusions after he had analysed 12 million company records held by Dun & Bradstreet. The first was that better access to funds was vital to these employment-generating smaller companies, especially while they were still in the vulnerable chrysalis stage. The snag there, he added, was that these companies were precisely 'the kind that banks feel very uncomfortable about'. His second observation was that small companies are also 'the kind most difficult to reach through conventional policy initiatives'. To sum it all up, Birch observed: 'We must learn to shoot with a rifle rather than a shotgun, if we are to be effective and non-inflationary. Rifle shooting requires a kind of knowledge that we simply have not had, and must obtain, if we are going to do it at all well.'

He could well have added that, irrespective of the weapon chosen, it is crucial to select the right target. The targets that American policymakers were shooting at during those rather panicky years of the 1970s are, to only a limited extent, the ones that Europeans should be aiming for in the 1980s. In the wake of Birch's study, another MIT expert, Professor Martin Rein, decided to take the whole investigation a stage further. Rein now suggests that the jobs boom was not a miraculous manifestation of America's grass roots capitalism working dynamically, but a form of once-removed government employment. In the same way that the development of education in America had been a hallmark of the 1950s and the growth in social services a sign of the sixties, Rein says, the expansion of health care was the job providing saviour of the 1970s.[16]

Birch's analysis gave the unwitting impression that the new jobs created were in self-sustaining 'market' activities, be they services such as fast foods or even manufacturing. It was an understandable gloss, for it was not easy for Rein later to trace how the nozzle of federal government money had in fact been injecting money into these new companies. It was a bit like tracing Mafia money back through the laundering process of the Cayman Islands' holding companies to the Panamanian banks to the casinos of the Bahamas. What had happened, however, was that, while visibly the federal government had been rapidly shedding people from its payroll, it had at the same time been paying over funds to state and local government for improved health services, that invisibly provided more employment than ever.

It was the American economy's inexplicable capacity for absorbing women into the workforce that first put Martin Rein on to the trail of the health industry boom. During the 1970s women accounted for 43 per cent of the labour force, as against only a third ten years before. At the same time federal employment, that in 1973 had mopped up a quarter of all those women, had by the latter 1970s sunk to only fourteen per cent. Yet they were not unemployed in the quantities that they should have been, so where had they gone? The answer, in many cases, was into government-funded 'private sector' medicine, such as the flourishing nursing homes industry. Social services, funded by the Medicare and Medicaid programmes, were generating over 800,000 new jobs a year.

Some European Commission officials, it so happens, believe that there should be a 'privatization' of medicine in many Community countries. EEC social affairs officials in Brussels like John Morley argue that a 'benign' transfer to private enterprise, not only of more health services but also of some education facilities, would by-pass Europe's hidebound public authorities and would inject job-creating vigour into those sectors.[17]

Even with the hindsight of American research, it is not easy to see what governments should be doing in the 1980s. Backing small businesses may well be one answer, but it should be approached with extreme caution. Health care, whatever else it is, remains a user of wealth not a generator, and, as an instrument of economic management, should be handled

gingerly. In manufacturing, where the new jobs should preferably be coming from, British experience has been that small
companies perform the least well in creating extra jobs.[18] Perhaps they are the ones where productivity improvements are the
least inhibited by restrictive practices, and so should be a model
to us all, but that in itself does not defuse the jobs crisis.

The UK's record in genuine job creation has so far been not
just poor but a textbook case study of what not to do. Some
estimates have put the cost to the taxpayer of a new industrial job
at £15,000,[19] which compares extremely badly with the figure of
$10,000 per job that former US Secretary of Labor Ray
Marshall reckons the Carter administration was spending.[20]
Worse still, it is now being suggested that only a small fraction of
British government spending aimed at boosting employment
ever hit the target – most of the pellets, in what MIT expert
David Birch would call the shotgun fusillade, missed and instead
stoked inflation. For between 1974–9, it has now been calculated, total spending by the state increased more than 120 per
cent, yet only ten per cent went towards raising output. The rest
raised prices by 110 per cent and so eventually helped raise
unemployment too.[21]

Chastening as that record is, no government, and least of all
the British government, can afford to do nothing in the face of a
jobs crisis that is turning progressively nasty. Possibly it is
Denmark that provides one of the best examples of a commonsense approach to public spending. In 1977 the Danes drew up
two lists, one of valid and high priority investment needs, the
other of job creation needs. Where items matched they went
right ahead, and now, more than $4 billion later, the Danish
authorities are convinced that they not only saved vital jobs, but
whole industries such as shipbuilding.

Inside HM Treasury in Whitehall there is a view that Britain
does not need new infrastructural improvements to any great
degree.[22] A spin north out of London along the M1 motorway, or
a crawl through the choked streets that serve the East End's
dockland, would be enough for most motorists to dispute that,

without undertaking a more detailed study of the beneficial impact on industrial costs in the 1990s of spending now on communications and energy-saving. In Paris, where planning and infrastructural development have long been the preserve of the Prime Minister's office, the Treasury's insouciance would raise more than a few eyebrows. The infrastructure built during the governmental chaos of the Fourth Republic laid the foundations for the industrial take-off of de Gaulle's Fifth Republic. British industry, with its tired alibi that the winning of World War II saddled it with old equipment, would do well to draw up two lists, Danish-style. As to the government's lists, it would be remarkable if housing did not figure prominently on both.

The Wages Wrangle

'We workers can't follow all this. You could write a book on it, it's so complicated.' Celestine Lovaert is a plump, blonde Flemish woman in her mid-forties who could have stepped straight out of a Breughel canvas. In 1980 she lost her job at the local Philips factory on the outskirts of the east Belgian market town of Hasselt. She remains to this day darkly suspicious of the Dutch electronics multi-national's investment strategies, and how they may favour jobs at the group's Eindhoven HQ across the border in Holland; but she is resigned to the technological facts of life that pushed her out of work, and will most probably keep her out.

'The modernization came much faster than people thought', she explains, 'faster than even the management expected.' For seven years her job had been to operate a machine producing audio cassettes, but, with the arrival of new techniques and equipment, the production unit she was in found itself cut from nine people to five. With a fairly perfunctory golden handshake of about £1000, Celestine, divorced mother of two, was out.

In Hasselt, people worry about the future of the Philips plant, for since the mid-1970s its payroll has dwindled from 5700 to 3400 and nobody knows if it won't close down entirely one day soon. They have good reason to feel concerned, for Philips still employs a quarter of a million workers in Europe, but is pinning its hopes for financial recovery on more drastic manpower pruning. It is not surprising in an industry beset by Japanese competition and in which, for example, the number of man hours needed to make a television set chassis has dropped from 22 in the early seventies to two today and will be down to just one tomorrow.

Celestine Lovaert's dispiriting experience is becoming an increasingly common one, and in the next few years semi-skilled workers such as she will be eased out of work at an accelerating rate by cheaper equipment. Her frank admission of ignorance as to the real reasons for her loss of livelihood reflects the widespread bewilderment that now exists. Her case also highlights the confusion that surrounds the whole question of industrial policy and employment theory.

Celestine lives in the heart of industrial Europe. The province of Limburg is the point where Belgium, Holland and West Germany meet, and Hasselt, like other nearby towns in all three countries has a well developed industrial estate in which a cross section of industries are present. She and her fellow Limburgers in effect provide a test bed in which different economic theories and developments can be measured.

So far, her experience has done little but raise questions to which there seem to be no answers. The first theory to emerge somewhat shaken must be that which is advanced by those who warn of the 'lump of labour' fallacy and argue that the streamlining of companies' labour forces will ultimately have a regenerative effect. The idea that, by making itself more competitive through new technology, Philips has become more profitable, or that through producing cheaper goods it can stimulate demand for them, has yet to be translated into fact.

The notion of re-generation of demand, thanks to the cost-cutting nature of micro-electronics, is an attractive one. Instead of being stuck in a dreary factory, the theory runs, people would be employed much more pleasantly in service industries because the great improvement in manufacturing productivity will have created a boom economy; instead of destroying jobs, technological advances 'transfer' them to other areas of the growing economy. An example of the way such efficiencies create work is civil aviation, which created tourism on a scale that compensated for lost jobs on passenger liners by a factor of thousands, and which created a service sector that dwarfs the aircraft manufacturing industry.

That greater efficiency is in itself a dynamic may turn out to be correct, but not yet in Hasselt. The theory that provides the basis for dreams of a 'post-industrial' society has still to harden into fact there, for Hasselt has seen no rise in services or new manufacturing jobs to compensate for the depradations of technology. It is, of course, a slow process, but Philips' own performance makes it clear that it is not one that governments should pin too many hopes on as a solution to the employment problems of the 1980s. Over the years, the Dutch giant's sales have risen steadily and are now approaching £1 billion a year. At the same time it has been shedding employees in the various countries where it operates at a rate of 10,000 a year. More goods are being turned out by fewer people, yet still it isn't enough. In the year that Celestine was sacked, Philip's net profits nosedived by 42 per cent, and anyone holding its shares got a miserable 2·7 per cent return on their money. So not only was the relationship between jobs and output being squeezed, but also Philips was paying out fewer wages and lower dividends to the potential customers for its products.

A place like Hasselt can provide an interesting insight into how general economic conditions work on the ground, but it is only fair to add that it risks being as instructive as studying a map through a microscope. On the other hand, economists who decry work-sharing and other palliatives such as early retirement, on the grounds that they perpetuate the lump of labour fallacy, have to date produced little enough in the way of practical measures for slowing joblessness. That the subject of unemployment should not have produced many breakthroughs in thinking during the post-war years of full employment is scarcely surprising. Now that it is the No. 1 problem, a welter of often contradictory diagnoses and cures is being put forward. At the same time, the onset of mass unemployment is beginning to shatter a number of hitherto unchallenged policies and assumptions in developed and developing countries alike.

China, which 'guarantees' full employment but today probably has some 20 million jobless,[1] is now coming to the con-clusion that its commitment to job security may in fact be aggrav-ating its unemployment problem. The People's Republic is already unequal to the task of finding work for 7 million school-leavers a year, and faces the prospect of a rise in its 1 billion population of at least another 200 million by the end of the century. Unemployment may well turn out to be one of the most serious threats to political stability there, particularly in cities such as Shanghai, and the Peking authorities now concede that the 'iron rice bowl', as lifetime employment by the state is known, should be abolished. The view is that its inefficiencies are in fact slowing down economic development and preventing the creation of more jobs.[2]

It is a conclusion that Western observers are also beginning to share as they review the effects of the various employment protection laws that were hailed in a number of countries as important social advances during the 1970s. In much the same way that employment schemes can have a low response rate because of the unwanted paperwork they impose on employers, the red tape, together with the constraints on dismissal, of employment protection and equal opportunity legislation is widely thought to be discouraging companies from expanding their payrolls, even when they may have good reason to do so.

The nub of the unemployment problem, though, is wages. Almost all economists now engaging in the increasingly heated debate over the sort of broad economic strategy needed to boost employment would agree with that. The trouble is that there is absolutely no agreement on whether the jobs crisis would be defused by a reduction in the level of wages. For wages do not only determine the cost, and therefore the competitiveness, of goods, they also affect the degree of demand there is for those goods. Put simply, a poorly-paid worker in, say, the glass industry would not be able to afford a new TV set, and by failing to buy a TV would not only depress the electronics industry but also would eventually reduce the amount of glass sold to the TV producers.

The counter-argument is, of course, that the industrialized

countries' high wages have been responsible for pricing their products out of the more toughly competitive sectors of the world market. It is claimed that if instead employers were to pay 'market clearing' wages – pay rates so low that workers would be pricing themselves back into work – then the joblessness trend would be reversed. The basic idea is that the prices of goods would be so much reduced that all workers, despite their own pay cuts, would be able to afford one another's products.

It is hard to see how those wage reductions could ever be so great as to achieve that desirable state of affairs. In international terms, the unit costs that the industrial countries must compete with will be the developing countries' combination of cheap labour and micro-technology. It is still more difficult to see how genuine pay restraint could be achieved, for even during the Great Depression of the 1930s real wages rose.

Yet the visions of a new prosperity that are being conjured up by some advocates of wage reductions should be compelling enough to make the strategy saleable to an electorate. Those in favour of wage-cutting say that if hourly pay rates were lower, then more hours a week might be worked. In that way, productivity would rise while incomes would be maintained at much the same level–in other words, people would simply work harder. The beneficial effects of that on the economy, it is said, would have a ripple effect; unemployment would fall, government spending to fund joblessness and counter industrial stagnation would be reduced, tax rates could be lowered and industrial investment encouraged.

If such a virtuous circle could be entered simply by the workforce deciding to accept temporary reductions in their real wages, then plainly it would be in its members' best interests to do so. The trouble is that the case for wage restraint is far from proven. Like so many economic theories, the argument is straightforward enough until confronted with unwelcome facts.

The classical view is that higher wages reduce employment, and the broad trend of the past ten years, say, would seem to bear that out. Real wages at the start of the seventies – meaning the cost to an employer of each employee – were just over £51 per week, and by the end of a decade had risen to around £61. (Both figures are calculated on 1975 constant prices to discount inflation.) In line with that rising earnings graph, unemployment has increased four-fold. The relationship between the wage growth and job loss figures, however, is riddled with contradictions that cast doubt over the theory as a whole. In 1973, for instance, wages made their sharpest single leap during the whole decade and increased by £2 a week, but total employment in the UK also rose by half a million and pushed the jobless figure from almost 900,000 to around 600,000. In 1976–77 the opposite happened, so that real wages actually dropped thirteen per cent while unemployment scarcely faltered in its advance from the 1 million mark to almost 1·5 million.[3]

Commonsense makes it obvious that there is nevertheless a good deal to be said for limiting wages growth, providing that demand is not strangled at the same time. A glance at Japan, where investment has been the top priority, with wages and therefore living standards following on, shows that it is possible, and in Britain a number of highly respected economists have been putting forward ideas on how to apply wage restraint. Politically, too, there seems to be a growing consensus on the issue, with the Labour Party's 'Shadow' Employment Secretary Eric Varley urging much the same pay discipline as does the Thatcher government.[4] At the same time, most politicians recognize that incomes policies of almost any sort are political dynamite, so it is unlikely that such pay restraint schemes as have been proposed by Nobel prizewinner Professor James Meade, that would be backed by a panoply of wage tribunals, will find much favour.

More subtle, in political terms at any rate, are the ideas now being put forward for using taxation as a flexible instrument for controlling pay rates. The device of striking umbrella wage restraint deals, or social contracts, with the trades unions is being seen as a focus for political friction, so that fiscal techniques are now the fashion. It is a long overdue development, for despite

the complexities of the tax regulations in most developed countries, fiscal policies as an instrument of economic management
are still used more like a bludgeon than a rapier.

A suggestion being made by the London School of Economics' Professor Richard Layard, and reportedly being looked
at by the SDP social democrats, is a tax that would penalize
employers if they award excessive pay rises. Like so many policy
proposals, it is not brand new; but it is an original variation on the
ideas for a 'taxed imposed incomes policy' – known in the jargon
as a TIP – that were much discussed inside the Carter administration in the US during the latter 1970s. Layard's plan involves a
heavy tax on employers who agree to wage rises over and above a
UK 'norm', so that as well as paying the extra in wages they
would be further handicapped by a punitively expensive levy. In
one example, an employer giving in to an £8 wages demand when
the norm being paid nationally is £5 would consequently suffer a
wage cost increase because of the tax of £11.

The new element in Layard's scheme is for the tax take to be
used to reduce the National Insurance contributions that all
employers pay, which makes it 'revenue neutral' and prevents it
from affecting the government's own finances. Insulating the
scheme to avoid a knock-on effect on the complicated factors
that determine management of the economy may well be a good
thing, but it has a major drawback. If all the employers stay
roughly in line on wage awards and simply ignore the norm
guidelines set out by government, then the system becomes
totally neutral with each company getting back in National Insurance reductions what it paid out in tax. For that reason, some
experts think that earlier versions of a TIP system in which
governments retained the tax would be better.

The attractive novelty of Layard's version remains that it is
effectively an 'inflation tax' that would damp down spiralling
wages without depressing demand and thus output. Any TIP that
is not revenue neutral would, on present showing, carry with it
the risk that the government's fiscal involvement would lead to a
squeeze on demand.

TIP-style schemes are not the only ones being advanced in Britain that seek to play a tune on the National Insurance system. One idea being strongly pushed is for the tax of National Insurance contributions that is paid by employers to be partially refunded to them as a way of subsidizing their wage costs. It therefore approaches the wages problem from the other direction. This suggestion for what is known as a payroll regulator has been around in one guise or another since at least 1944, but could be an idea whose time has come. It has a number of practical advantages, such as involving no great administrative re-organization, and is also politically quite uncontentious.

In economic terms, the argument is that, by reducing the government's tax take, the rebate would have little effect on the inflation rate while encouraging companies to maintain, or even increase, their workforces. There are a number of other suggestions for using National Insurance as a flexible fiscal instrument to promote employment, and all share the general argument that the government would be able to recoup the revenue it loses through the rising tax income that would follow a fall in unemployment.

Whatever the details of the different schemes, there seems an overriding argument in favour of an imaginative revamp of taxation policies. The tax structure could provide the most versatile means of hitting at the jobs crisis; it is a built-in, fast-working mechanism for influencing both corporate and personal behaviour, and can often by-pass the much more cumbersome use of cash subsidies.

By the same token, the use of taxation to cut through the inconsistencies of dole payments and other associated benefits is also worth examination. It would help counter the problems of unemployment benefit being only a short term insurance system, when in future it will clearly be required to become a long term incomes system.

The concept of a negative income tax, such as put forward not long ago by Professor Victoria Curzon Price of the University of Geneva, has the great advantage over standard welfare benefits of not being a great magnet to unemployment. The idea is that a poverty line is established, and those people who legitimately earn less than that are paid an 'income tax' by the state, while those who earn more pay tax to the state. The key proviso is that, as the earned income of those below the line rises, the 'amount of aid received from the state would diminish; but by less than the increase in earned income. Thus, their total income would rise the more they earned themselves.'[5] In other words, the scheme has the major plus point of not locking the unemployed into any of the poverty traps created by rigid benefit systems that preclude people from doing any work at all, other than illegally in the black economy.

Variations on the negative income tax theme could also be used to ensure that high income taxpayers, whose redundancies tend to be overlooked as a problem, could also more easily recoup their formerly high contributions. Encouraging that is not only a question of equity, it also has a practical value as it would make the launching of new small businesses by entrepreneurs more likely.

There seems little disagreement between the experts that reforms to the unemployment and social security benefit system in the UK, as elsewhere, are overdue, and could have an appreciable effect on the jobless levels. Where they differ, naturally, is over what those reforms should be. Some believe the policing of the benefits should be more stringent, in order to discourage voluntary unemployment, while others suggest increasing the non-employment benefits so as to shrink the importance to poor families of the dole itself.

That was one of the chief proposals made by Professor Patrick Minford of Liverpool University in a policy package that aimed to cut UK unemployment by 1·22 million people by 1984–5 at a net cost of about £5 billion. He suggested that child benefits should be increased by £2 a head, and as a complement to that a ceiling should be set on benefits to the unemployed of 75 per cent of net household earnings when that unemployed person was in work. The package consists of a variety of other carrot-and-stick approaches, such as raising council house rents to private sector levels to encourage labour mobility, and helping to pay for that apparent paradox by tinkering with and lowering income tax thresholds and bands. Minford also favours reducing National Insurance contributions by employers, and perhaps the most interesting assertion in his plan is the effect that stimulating output and employment would have on offsetting the cost of the measures. The gross cost to the government's borrowing requirement, at 1981 prices, is calculated at £11·2 billion, but, when the pick-up in the economy produced by putting well over 1 million unemployed back to work is subtracted, the net cost comes down to £5·1 billion.

That is far from being the most controversial of his ideas, though. For he has argued that real demand for labour can be increased by radical trades union reforms. He urges the now familiar moves to reduce the unions' power of making the closed shop illegal and removing the immunity they won in 1906 from actions for damages. Union-bashing, which Minford claimed would have a cash advantage to the economy of some £2 billion-plus by the mid-eighties as it would prevent young jobseekers from being priced out of work by high wage deals, nevertheless poses a number of wider questions.

During the 1980s, wages and organized labour's power to set them, in defiance of a labour market in which supply is outstripping demand, will evidently be a key political issue. It is also one whose outcome should provide a significant pointer to the social structure that the much heralded 'post-industrial' society will bring with it. The behaviour of the trades unions is undoubtedly going to be a vital factor.

In Britain, as in other industrialized countries, it is still far from clear whether the unions see their most important constituency as being the employed or the unemployed. They argue, of course, that there can be no distinction as they represent their memberships, irrespective of whether they are in or out of work.

John Maynard Keynes, the pre-eminent British economist whose theories on the advantages of stimulating demand dominated policy-making for almost 50 years, was under few illusions. Back in the 1920s, Keynes observed that when it came down to a choice between more unemployment or a cut in wages, the British working man and his union would in effect opt for higher joblessness by refusing the wage cuts. That, indeed, is precisely what is happening today. The powerful trades unions representing skilled workforces have been pressing home wage demands at the expense of workers in less skilled trades who are more vulnerable to unemployment.

So far, the unions' general thinking does not appear to have developed to take account of the structural changes to their position being produced by the jobs crisis. Their policy has been to demand, somewhat plaintively, that governments should reflate, while lowering productivity through worksharing, and so restore employment to pre-crisis levels. It is a fall back on wishful thinking that suggests no contingency plans are being laid for the concessions that trade unionists will need to make. Yet it is not only the likely long term surplus of labour that will be eroding their traditional monopoly powers. There is also the international dimension of the problem that will be greatly weakening their power base.

It has been calculated that, in the highly competitive sectors of the newly industrialized countries, the supply of people with engineering skills will so outpace demand that pay rates there will actually keep on dropping from now until well into the twenty-first century. Prophecies like that are even more suspect than economists' projections, but it is certainly true that the skilled crafts that are the core of union power in developed countries will be caught between cheap foreign labour and cheap micro-electronic technology.

The micro-chip provides employment for qualified technicians and for the unskilled; it is the skills of engineering craftsmen that it reproduces. If they could, the trades unions would no doubt be prepared to continue trading high unemployment among the less skilled trades in return for higher wages for their skilled members. But it looks as if they will not be able to do so. With the balance of advantage now moving steadily against them, the signs are that, after all the political victories of the twentieth century, the unions will lose the war unless they negotiate a peace.

But riding roughshod over labour, once the monopoly of the trades unions is weakened, is no answer to the social problems of high unemployment. It is more like a formula for bloody revolution. Before attempting to turn the screw on wages, governments might even do well to reassess not how low they should be, but how high.

The inflation versus employment debate is beginning to shed some light, at last, on the rather obscure relationship between the two. That they present no more than a straightforward dilemma to governments has been seen as pretty suspect for some time, except perhaps by some governments. But as there undeniably is an important link, it is inflation itself that is now considered by some analysts to be long overdue for a re-think.

Almost everyone agrees that, in theory, there would be no great problem with inflation if all the competing economies of the leading industrial countries were to be inflating at much the same rate. But that is about as likely as a handicapper's vision of a perfect horse race, in which all the runners would cross the finishing line in a dead heat. Yet, on closer inspection, inflation may not even be quite as villainous a creature as it is always said to be. Not long ago, *Financial Times* economic commentator Anthony Harris raised a number of interesting questions that challenged some very old prejudices about inflation. Although inflation is universally recognized as an economic evil, he pointed out that 'there is no evidence at all that inflation inhibits growth'. He was not arguing that it should be treated in any cavalier fashion, or indeed that it was a great strength of Germany's Weimar Republic in the 1920s that the workers should turn up with wheelbarrows twice a day to be paid in bundles of almost worthless million mark notes; only that inflation and growth are very different things, but can coincide.

Harris also pointed out that inflation is a mechanism for redistributing wealth. Although it is always said to hit the poor the hardest, it happens, too, to force the readjustment of low incomes to keep them more or less in line with the wage increases being earned by top-notch factory workers.[6] When it comes down to it, inflation is like fissionable nuclear matter. Providing its reaction is carefully controlled, it may even provide a source of energy. It is certainly true that the clod-hopping techniques used to stamp out inflation also have the effect of stamping out growth.

Inflation at an even and fairly predictable rate is a factor that most businesses can cope with. It is the violent hiccups in inflation that do the real damage. In the first place, they upset the delicate structure of wages deals in different industries, and of price levels, and that has a knock-on effect of reducing demand. More fundamental still, the uncertainty created by yo-yoing inflation rates is starving industry of long term investment funds. Lenders are wary of sinking money into a venture on terms that may turn out to be punitive a few years hence, and so the desirable cycle of investment-production-consumption-investment is slowing down. It has instead turned into a vicious circle, for, if the average industrial share in Britain were to have yielded a reasonably healthy profit over the past ten years, it has been reckoned that the FT index would now be at about 1300 instead of stagnating around the 500 mark. The less attractive a proposition share-buying becomes, the less profitable will capital-starved companies be. In that way, the distinction between inflation and growth does become sadly clearer.

One answer must, surely, be to revive the idea of paying workers in the shares of the company they work for, as well as in cash. It was a very voguish innovation about ten years ago, when it was rather unattractively called 'asset formation', but has largely died a death since then. Chiefly, it is said, because managements did not support a mechanism that was becoming inextricably intertwined with the more vexed issue of worker participation in decision making. It was also, to be fair, less attractive then to employees than it would be now because real earnings were rising steadily. There was little incentive to accept part-payment in share certificates of a generally non-negotiable nature.

But rewarding valued workers through a system that gives them an undoubted longer term stake in their company's performance, which does not immediately exacerbate inflation, which promotes vital new investment in plant and equipment and which increases the wealth and collateral borrowing power of the employee, must make sense.

If sound sense and nonsense, commonsense and misapprehensions that are merely commonplace, could all be neatly winnowed into their different categories, then a strategy for counter-attacking the tide of unemployment might emerge that much more quickly. As it is, both the causes and the effects of widespread joblessness are obscure: the causes because there is almost too much information, the effects because there is still too little.

Many governments like to view the jobs crisis as an avalanche – an unavoidable onslaught that will stop as suddenly as it started, and from which the Western economies will soon be able to dig themselves out. The more realistic analysis is that it is a glacier, which beneath its surface is gouging away at our familiar economic, social and political structures just as savagely as the glaciers that once landscaped the earth.

REFERENCES

CHAPTER 1
The Blighted Generation

1 OECD member states: Australia, Austria, Belgium, Canada, Denmark, Finland, France, Greece, Iceland, Ireland, Italy, Japan, Luxembourg, the Netherlands, New Zealand, Norway, Portugal, Spain, Sweden, Switzerland, Turkey, West Germany, United Kingdom, United States.

2 David Lea, TUC, in conversation, June 1981.

3 Christopher Brooks, OECD Secretariat, in conversation, June 1981.

4 European Trade Union Confederation: Manifesto for Employment and Economic Recovery (Brussels, June 1980).

5 'The Jobs Crisis – Increasing Unemployment in the Developed World', Harry Shutt, Economist Intelligence Unit Special Report No. 85 (London, September 1980).

6 'Global Employment and Economic Justice: the Policy Challenge', Kathleen Newland, *Worldwatch Paper* 28 (Washington DC, April 1979).

7 *Guardian*, Michael Shanks, 13 May 1981.

8 *The Zero-Sum Society – Distribution and the Possibilities for Economic Change*, Lester Thurow (Penguin Books, 1981), p. 203.

9 'Micro-processors, Luddites and their Economic Consequences', Sir Ieuan Maddock, *The World Economy*, 1980.

10 Ray Marshall, in conversation, May 1981.

CHAPTER 2
Those Fallible Forecasters

1 'The Economic Implications of Demographic Change in the European Community: 1975–95'. Part 1. Report to the European Commission, June 1978.

2 *Economist*, 21 October 1978.

3 Gary Stern, of New York economic consultant A. Gary Shilling & Co., in conversation, May 1981.

4 *International Herald Tribune*, Axel Krause, 23 May 1981.

5 *Business Week*, 20 April 1981.

6 *Economist*, 19 August 1978.

7 W. van Ginneken, International Labour Office in *International Labour Review*, vol. 120, No. 2, March/April 1981.

8 Len Murray, TUC General Secretary, and David Lea, Assistant General Secretary, in conversation, June 1981.

9 James Prior, in conversation, June 1981.

10 W. W. Daniel, 'Why is High Unemployment Somehow Still Acceptable?', *New Society*, 19 March 1981.

11 De-classified memorandum from Sir Richard O'Brien, Chairman Manpower Services Commission, to National Economic Development Council.

12 ibid.

13 *Eurostat*, monthly unemployment bulletin, May 1981.

14 Jacques Rigaudiat, Commissariat au Plan, in conversation, June 1981.

CHAPTER 3
The Disintegrating Industrial Jalopy

1 *European Industrial Policy:* Report to EFTA on economic policies which affect industrial structure and trade by the European Trade Union Institute (Brussels, April 1981), pp 4–5.

2 *Economist*, 8 November 1980.

3 ibid.

4 *Restructuring of Industrial Economies and Trade with Developing Countries,* Santosh Mukherjee, International Labour Office, 1978.

5 ibid. *See also* ETUI *European Industrial Policy,* op. cit., p. 7.

6 ETUI Report, op. cit., p. 10.

7 *Economist*, 19 August 1978.

8 Report of the Mayor of Detroit, Coleman Young, 1980–1.

9 'Demographics and American Economic Policy'. Paper by Peter F. Drucker delivered 22 March 1981 to the Wharton School of the University of Pennsylvania.

10 ibid.

11 Eli Ginzberg, in conversation, May 1981.

12 'The Western European

Automotive Industry: Where Now in the 1980s?', Economist Intelligence Unit, May 1980.

13 *Financial Times*, Terry Dodsworth, 6 March 1978.

14 *Financial Times*, Kenneth Gooding, 25 November 1980.

15 *Business Week*, 10 November 1980.

16 *Financial Times*, Kenneth Gooding, 4 June 1981.

17 ETUI Report, op. cit., pp. 185–6.

18 *Economist*, 25 April 1981.

CHAPTER 4
The Micro-electronics Monster

1 European Commission, February 1980, communication to the Standing Employment Committee: 'Employment and the New Micro-electronic Technology', Annex P. 1.

2 European Trade Union Institute, Brussels 1980, 'The Impact of Micro-electronics on Employment in Western Europe in the 1980s', para. 190.

3 European Commission, 1980, Annex P. 6. op. cit.

4 ETUI, 1980, quoting Lamborghini, 'The Diffusion of Micro-electronics in Industrial Companies'.

5 UK Post Office Engineering Union, 'The Modernisation of Communications', 1979.

6 *The Manpower Implications of Micro-electronic Technology* (HMSO, 1979).

7 European Commission, 1980, Annex P. 7. op. cit.

8   ETUI, 1980, para. 195. op. cit.

9   PTTI Studies, 1978, 'Trade Unions and the New Technology in Posts and Telecommunications'.

10   Bernard Bruhnes, Hôtel Matignon, in conversation with the author, June 1981.

11   Metra Consulting, 'The Impact of Chip Technology on Employment and the Labour Market', (Netherlands, 1979).

12   ETUI, 1980, para. 216. op. cit.

13   'Micro-processors, Luddites and their Economic Consequences', Sir Ieuan Maddock, *The World Economy*, 1980.

14   ETUI, 1980, para. 55, quoting Barron and Curnow, *The Future with Micro-electronics* (Francis Pinter, 1979).

15   *Economist*, 3 January 1981.

16   ETUI, 1980, para. 202. op. cit.

17   *Office 1990*, Siemens, quoted by Friederichs: 'New Dimensions of Automation and Technical Change by Micro-electronics', 1979.

18   European Commission, 1980, Annex P. 8 quoting ILO (Geneva, 1979).

19   APEX, 'Office Technology', 1979.

20   FIET, Report on the Trade Section Conference of Salaried Employees in Industry (Geneva, 1979).

21   IRIS, 'Automation, travail et emploi', Universite de Paris Dauphine, 1979.

22   ETUI, 1980, para. 212. op. cit.

23   European Commission, 1980, Annex P. 9.

24   *Financial Times*, 21 March 1981.

25   *L'Informatisation de la Societe, La Documentation Francaise*, Simon Nora & Alain Minc, 1978.

26   *The Times*, June 1981.

27   Maddock, op. cit.

28   'Demographics and American Economic Policy', Peter F. Drucker to the Wharton School of the University of Pennsylvania, 1981.

29   ETUI, 1980, para. 207. op. cit.

30   *idem*, para. 244.

31   *idem*, para. 218.

32   European Commission, 1980, Annex P. 4, quoting *Bientot 7 Millions de Chomeurs*, P. Berger, Informatique et Gestion, 1977.

33   European Commission, 1980, Annex P. 4. op. cit.

34   *The Collapse of Work*, Jenkins & Sherman (Eyre Methuen, 1979).

35   OECD Committee on Science and Technology: 'Science and Technology in the New Socio-economic Context'.

CHAPTER 5
Of Scroungers and Suicides

1   *The Times*, Pat Healy, 20 May 1981.

2   *The Times*, David Piachaud, 27 May 1981.

3   'Economic Responsibilities of Working Women', US Department of Labor.

4   *The Times*, 20 May 1981, op. cit.

5   *US News & World Report*, 23 June 1980.

6   ibid.

7   *Observer*.

8   *US News & World Report*, op. cit.

9   *The Times*, 6 June 1981.

10   *US News & World Report*, op. cit.

11   'Youth, Work and Unemployment', Paul Osterman, *Challenge*, May-June 1978.

12   Michael Piore, in conversation, May 1981.

13   *The Times*, Frances Williams, 20 May 1981.

14   *New Society*, Alan Deacon, 28 February 1980.

15   *Time* magazine, 11 August 1980.

16   *The Times*, 24 September 1980.

17   *The Times*, 27 May 1981, op. cit.

18   *Economist*, 6 June 1981.

19   *The Times*, 26 February 1981.

20   Lester Thurow, in conversation, May 1981.

21   *Time* magazine, 11 August 1980, op. cit.

22   *Financial Times*, David Buchan, 10 March 1981.

23   *Knight News Service*, Aaron Epstein, March 1981.

24   *New York Times*, 7 March 1981.

25   *Our Secret Economy*, Graeme Shankland (Anglo-German Foundation, 1980).

26   *The Times*, 11 August 1980.

27   'Employment Goals and the World Plan of Action: Developments in the US'. Report by the US Department of Labor, July 1980.

28   Market & Opinion Research International, September 1979.

CHAPTER 6
Politics and Violence: the Critical Threshold

1   *Le Point,* 5 February 1979.

2   Len Murray, in conversation, June 1981.

3   *L'Express*, 10 February 1979.

4   *Financial Times*, 13 January 1981.

5   ibid., 24 December 1980.

6   *International Herald Tribune*, 29 December 1980.

7   *Los Angeles Times*, 10 May 1981.

8   *Financial Times*, 21 February 1980.

9   James Prior, in conversation, June 1981.

10   *Report on the National Advisory Commission on Civil Disorders* (Bantam Books, New York, March 1968).

11   *The Times*, 13 April 1981.

12   Pacific News Service, Report No. 491981.

13   ibid.

14   *The Times*, 13 April 1981.

15   *Financial Times*, 23 March 1981.

16   *Financial Times*, 24 May 1981.

17   *Financial Times*, 13 January 1981.

18   Internal MSC Report shown to author, 2 June 1981.

19   Pacific News Service, Report No. 5221980.

20   *Economist*, 21 March 1981.

21   *Washington Post*, 27 April 1981.

22   *Economist*, 16 May 1981.

23   *Economist*, 21 March 1981.

24   *New Statesman*, March 1981.

25 Robert Worcester, in conversation, June 1981.

26 *British Public Opinion* journal, autumn 1979.

27 *Economist*, 16 May 1981.

28 *The Times*, 24 June 1981.

29 Declaration de M. Delors au Conseil au niveau des Ministres OCDE, document à diffusion restreinte, 17 June 1981.

30 *The Times*, 22 May 1981.

31 *The Times*, 23 May 1981.

32 *The Slump – Society and Politics during the Depression*, John Stevenson & Chris Cook (Jonathan Cape, 1977).

33 *The Times*, 27 May 1981.

34 Bernard Bruhnes, Hôtel Matignon, in conversation, June 1981.

CHAPTER 7
Trade Wars and Worse

1 *Economist*, 3 January 1981.

2 *North-South: A Programme for Survival.* Report on the Independent Commission on International Development Issues under the Chairmanship of Willy Brandt (Pan Books, London).

3 *Employment, Trade and North-South Co-operation*, edited by Geoffrey Renshaw, International Labour Office, Geneva.

4 Henry Wallach, in conversation, April 1981.

5 *Restructuring of Industrial Economies and Trade with Developing Countries*, Santosh Mukherjee, International Labour Office, Geneva, p. 23.

6 'EEC Protectionism: Present Practice and Future Trends', Noelke & Taylor, 1981.

7 Mukherjee, op. cit., p. 28.

8 *Background Report* No. 92, House of Commons Library Research Division, 19 March 1981, p. 3.

9 Lester Thurow, in conversation, May 1981.

10 *Eastern Industrialization and its Effect on the West*, G. E. Hubbard (Greenwood Press, Connecticut), p. 5.

11 *Misunderstanding – Europe v Japan*, Endymion Wilkinson (Chokoron-Sha, Tokyo), p. 185.

12 ibid, pp. 184, 228.

13 ibid, p. 184.

14 *The Pacific War*, Saburo Ienaga (Pantheon Books, New York), p. 153.

15 ibid, p. 79.

16 Noelke & Taylor, European Research Associates, op. cit.

17 Office of the Mayor, Detroit, Michigan, May 1981.

18 Noelke & Taylor, op. cit.

19 'The Impact of Micro-electronics on Employment in Western Europe in the 1980s', European Trade Union Institute (Brussels 1980), para. 162.

20 Wilkinson, op. cit., p. 230.

21 *Trade Problems between Japan and Western Europe*, Masamichi Hanabusa (Saxon House), p. 83.

22 *The Pacific War*, op. cit., p. 255.

23 *International Herald Tribune*, 16 September 1980. Japan's Debate on Security, Kenneth L. Adelman, Strategic Studies Center, SRI International.

24 *Economist*, 25 April 1981, pp. 109–11.

25 'The Coming Trade War at Home', Jeff Frieden, *The Nation*, 18 April 1981.

26 *Financial Times*, 26 May 1981.

27 *Background Report* No. 92, House of Commons, op. cit., pp. 9–10.

28 Noelke & Taylor, op. cit.

29 *Financial Times*, 22 June 1981.

30 *North-South*, Brandt Report, op. cit., pp. 14, 120.

CHAPTER 8
Make-work Schemes – Miracles or Mirage?

1 Surface area $500 billion = approx. 40 sq. kms. Europe = 9·74 sq. kms. Africa = 29·88 sq. kms.

2 Leon Brittan, HC Deb., 29 January 1981. *Hansard*, col. 1058.

3 *Financial Times*, 15 January 1981.

4 Lord Cockfield, HL Deb., 2 March 1981, *Hansard*, col. 1216.

5 *Employment Policy Alternatives to Unemployment in the Federal Republic of Germany*, Lutz Reyher, Martin Koller and Eugen Spitznagel (Nuremberg, April 1979), pp. 58–62.

6 'The European Economy 1980–85: An Indicative Full-Employment Plan', European Trade Union Institute (Brussels, June 1980), p. 11.

7 'The Conflict over Working Hours', Klaus Vater, Inter Nationes (Bonn, June 1980), pp. 6–14.

8 *The Reduction of Working Hours in Western Europe*. Second Part: 'Analysis of the Social and Economic Consequences', European Trade Union Institute (Brussels, May 1980), p. 30.

9 'Working Time Reductions and Unemployment', the Conference Board in Europe (Brussels, 1981). pp. 30–31.

10 ibid, p. 20.

11 ETUI *Reduction of Working Hours* Report, op. cit., p. 37.

12 Conference Board Report, op. cit., p. 20.

13 ETUI *Reduction of Working Hours* Report, op. cit., pp. 42–4.

14 *Selective Employment Policy to Stimulate Economic Recovery: an Evaluation of the German Federal Republic Program for Regions with Special Employment Problems*, Günther Schmid, Wissenschaftszentrum (Berlin, 1981).

15 James Prior, in conversation. June 1981.

16 *Financial Times*, 23 June 1981.

17 *The Times*, 3 December 1980.

18 *Financial Times*, 2 September 1980.

19 *The Times*, 30 March 1981.

20 *The Times*, 2 June 1981.

21 *Guardian*, 7 July 1981.

22 *The Times*, 19 March 1981.

23 *Wall Street Journal*, May 1981.

24 *The Times*, 16 December 1980.

CHAPTER 9
Job Creation and Construction

1 *The Times*, Louis Heren, 19 May 1981.

2 *Unemployment*, Kevin Hawkins (Penguin Books, 1979), p. 69.

3 *New York Times*, 27 July 1980.

4 'Public Finance Measures to Generate Employment for

Hard-to-Place People', Günther Schmid, International Institute of Management (Berlin, 1980).

5 *Washington Post*, 2 May 1981.

6 *Financial Times*, Samuel Brittan, 30 April 1981.

7 'Background to Regional Policy', memorandum by the Director General, National Economic Development Council, London 1981.

8 *The Times*, Nicholas Timmins, 5 September 1980.

9 *Economist*, 1 August 1981.

10 Franco Modigliani, in conversation, May 1981. *see also New Mortgage Designs for Stable Housing in an Inflationary Environment*, Federal Reserve Bank of Boston, January 1975.

11 *Financial Times*, David Lascelles, 29 May 1981.

12 *Time* magazine, 17 August 1981.

13 *The Times*, John Huxley, June 1981.

14 'The Development of Labour Market Policy in Sweden and in Germany: Competing or Convergent Models to Combat Unemployment?'. Jan Johannesson, Swedish Ministry of Labour, and Günther Schmid, Wissenschaftzentrum, Berlin (Elsevier Scientific Publishing, Amsterdam, 1980).

15 'The Job Generation Process', David L. Birch, MIT Program on Neighbourhood and Regional Change (Cambridge, Mass. 1979).

16 Martin Rein, in conversation, May 1981.

17 John Morley, in conversation, June 1981.

18 'Job Generation in Scottish Manufacturing Industry', University of Strathclyde (Glasgow, 1981).

19 *Financial Times*, John Elliott, 25 June 1981.

20 Ray Marshall, in conversation, May 1981.

21 *How to End the 'Monetarist' Controversy*, Samuel Brittan, Institute of Economic Affairs, London 1981.

22 Ian Byatt, HM Treasury, in conversation, June 1981.

CHAPTER 10

The Wages Wrangle

1 *Financial Times*, Tony Walker, 10 November 1981.

2 *Financial Times*, Colina MacDougal, 8 January 1982.

3 *Guardian*, Christopher Huhne, 5 January 1982.

4 Eric Varley, in conversation, June 1981.

5 International Labour Office Review, April 1981.

6 *Financial Times*, Anthony Harris, 25 June 1981.

INDEX

Pahl, Ray, 83, 84
Phillips, A. W., 176
Piachaud, David, 89
Piore, Michael, 110
Player, David, 82
Police: strengths, 106; methods and
civil disorders, 104, 105;
'Operation Swamp', 106; and
community, 107, 108; recruitment
of blacks, 107
Policy Studies Institute (UK), 81,
83, 87, 90
Prior, James, 35, 104, 163
Productivity: effects of word
processor on clerical employment,
69; of Japanese, European and US
motor manufacturers, 132; traded
for jobs, 29, 30; US decline of, 29;
in UK ship-building, 56; as an
element of work-sharing, 156
Prognos, 26, 61, 74
Protectionism: !nancial techniques,
142; EEC motor industry, 133;
European Research Associates
report, 130, 142; inflationary
effects, 19

Racial minorities, as scapegoats, 99,
103; in Europe, 104; in US, 105,
110
Reagan administration, 14, 110, 138,
140, 141, 146; pressure for
'workfare', 170, 171
Rein, Martin, 194, 195
Retailing, job losses in, 73
Richard, Ivor, 32
Royal Institute of International
Affairs (*see* Chatham House)

Scarman, Lord, 104
Schmidt, Helmut, 113, 141
SDP (Social Democratic Party), 113,
114; and taxation policy, 204
Service sector, 7; jobs created in, 44;
function of, 52
Sherman, Barrie, 74

Ship-building, decline of industry,
45; as generator of more jobs, 56;
government subsidy of, 169; job
losses in EEC, 57
Siemens, 67, 69
Slavery, of children, 94
Small companies, as job creators,
193, 194, 195
SMMT (Society of Motor
Manufacturers and Traders –
UK), 142
Social security, effects of cuts in US,
110; and unemployment benefit in
France, 75; and unemployment
benefits, reform of, in UK, 206,
207
Southwark, 163
Soviet Union, 126, 144, 146
Spain, auto industry, 53; General
Motors, 134
Steed, Michael, 113, 115
Steel, decline of industry, 45, 53;
Italian non-tariff barriers against
German shipments, 142; job losses
in Europe, 54, 55; Longwy riots,
100, 101; overcapacity of industry
in Europe and projections, 56;
subsidised losses, 55; threatened
W. German import controls, 141
Stonier, Tom, 167
Sumitomo Bank, 137
Sweden: Academy of Engineering
Sciences, 59; economic
deterioration, 60; effects of public
subsidies on unemployment, 59;
Industrial Economic Research
Institute, 59; job creation
measures, 191; Public housing
'starts', 183; use of robots in auto
industry, 68
Switzerland, housing shortage, 179;
protest movement, 111

Taxation, 203, 204, 207; and black
economy, 206; 'inflation tax', 204;
need for revamp in policies of,